DREAM OF A LIFETIME

DREAM OF A LIFETIME

TEN YEARS IN THE UPPER AMAZON

NORMAN WALTERS

Book Design & Production: Columbus Publishing Lab
www.ColumbusPublishingLab.com

Published internationally by
Yacumama Press
644 NW 18th Street
Homestead, Florida 33030
www.yacumamalodge.net

Copyright 2019 by Norman E. Walters

All rights reserved. This book, or parts thereof, may not be reproduced in any form without permission.

LCCN: 2019931671
Paperback ISBN: 978-1-63337-249-8
E-book ISBN: 978-1-63337-250-4

Printed in the United States of America
1 3 5 7 9 10 8 6 4 2

*DEDICATED TO THE ONES I LOVE,
AND TO ALL "UNSUNG HEROES"*

You hear stories of "unsung heroes" in faraway corners of the world and think of bravery, selflessness, and inspiration. There is always admiration for their deeds. I would like to share a mixed bag of tales from my corner of the world, the incredible Peruvian Amazon Rainforest, and along the way, garnish them with exotic spices.

This is an accounting of events that has been created by many experiences in my life. I depict myself as I am, but other characters may resemble people you know or have heard of. This was not my intention, and any likeness is the result of coincidence only (unless it was my intention). Some scenes may not be in the correct sequence, or may have been tweaked in order to be presented properly. I guess you can take that as artistic freedom in the memoirs of an old man.

AUTHOR'S NOTE

When I first heard the proposition—a real-life Swiss Family adventure in the last days of the twentieth century on a remote river, deep in the Peruvian Amazon Rainforest—I knew it was just what the doctor ordered.

My last real adventure had been almost twenty years before (1973). My music partner, Jimmy (the other half of our music duo Wind and Cloud), and I had taken a break on Maui after a bit of recording in San Francisco.

When he went back to the grind, I stayed on Maui, got married, had kids (delivering them at home), organically farmed an old, seven-tiered taro plantation (you know, carving out our existence with the sun, wind, rain, waterfalls, bananas, papayas, mangos, avocados, in the presence of the Great Spirit), created Unity Circle of Friends, the natural food co-op on Maui, and The Makena Beach Clean-Up Project (supported by locals and hippies working together), studied religion in the Far East, divorced, was a single father, was almost persuaded to run for mayor, got "island fever," and moved the whole famn damily to Florida, my mom included (1981).

1981-1992: I call this time my "Zombie Diaries." My time of struggle, pain, and loss. I may refer to these years, but I will not bore you by writing about them. Four different companies, in Florida, Lake Tahoe, marriage, Marin County, Reno, divorce, and Florida again. That is my story, and I am sticking to it.

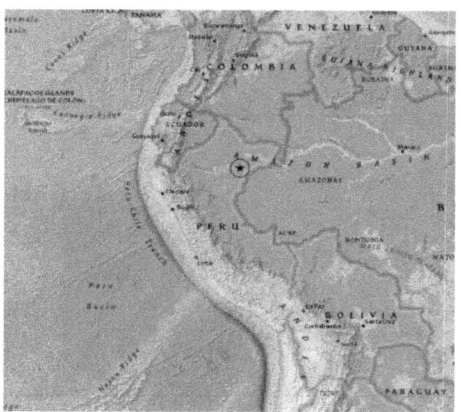

This story will be based in the Upper Amazon of Peru, where we were building an ecological tourist destination. We named the lodge, with the help of our local villagers, Yacumama Lodge. The Yacumama (giant anaconda, or boa) is the mother of the water—its protector, and guardian.

I'll also sprinkle in a little bit of New York, California, Hawaii, and the Far East, just to jazz it up a bit.

- PART I -
UNSUNG HEROES

Brazil, Hawaii, and Florida
1992

CHAPTER ONE

August 1992, Florida: One of the most difficult months to be a resident due to all the sand flies, mosquitos, sea lice, red tide, jellyfish, and sharks fiercely competing to keep me off the beach and out of the water, which was the only escape from the stifling heat and humidity. (And I guess I was a resident, seeing as how I had been in Florida, again, for almost six months. I wanted to be close to my ill mother, and I was escaping an eleven-year dysfunctional relationship.)

As I sat drinking my morning coffee on my screened-in porch (trying to combat the no-see-ums), scheming a way to be anywhere but there, the phone rang.

Jarred from my reverie, I lifted the receiver, expecting a panicked client with another domestic emergency. I was pleasantly surprised to hear the voice of my old mate Larry, whom I hadn't spoken with in about three years (although time has no bearing on when, where, or how long for those who have unraveled the fabric of reality). I heard, "What are you doing way down there in the South?"

We'd been friends since high school and had done just about everything you could think of that was out of the ordinary. In the late '60s we played music in Central Park, Washington Square, and Greenwich Village, went to Woodstock, hitchhiked from NYC to

San Fran and around the US, homesteaded in West Virginia, lived in tepees, built log cabins, and organic truck farmed in the lush jungle valleys of Maui.

Then he went his way and I went mine, to raise families and live life for the next ten years or so—my Zombie Diaries. Come to find out, my old buddy had been busy the prior year. He'd been working on putting together an eco-friendly tourist facility in Peru in the Amazon Rainforest. Supposedly, he had purchased about 50,000 hectares of pristine jungle on the first feeding tributary into the Río Amazonas (Amazon River).

Hmm, I was getting interested. He'd paid a ridiculously small price per acre to an American woman, brokering it for a Peruvian man. This woman had a small lodge next to the land he was purchasing, and she protected the pink dolphins. Did you know there are only two rivers in the world where the pink river dolphins choose to live, the Río Amazonas and the Ganges, in India?

This is when Larry asked me if I was free to work on the project with him. I've got to tell you, it was getting to me, but I was still reluctant because neither of us spoke Spanish except *hola* (hi), *chicas lindas* (cute girls), and, *quesiera bailar conmigo* (would you like to dance with me?). You get the picture? So he went on and on, unraveling this incredible ball of yarn.

The American woman, we'll call her Dolphin Lady, or maybe the DL (and we may as well change Larry's name to Lawrence, because at this point in time he was introducing himself as such), invited Lawrence as a guest to the Earth Summit '92 in Rio de Janeiro, Brazil. Remember Al Gore and the world's elite, talking about what to do with the lands of the indigenous natives? When Lawrence arrived, he realized that there were no indigenous tribal members slated to speak before the summit, but there was another "Native" summit about fifty kilometers away. This was the place for the natives to talk and come to their own resolutions — we had the bases covered, right?

Lawrence told me he rented a bus, had it driven to the "Native" summit, invited (this was all with an interpreter, of course) a bunch of chiefs to come aboard, and explained his plan to them. They were all for it. He stormed the gates of the Rio Summit and was met by an array of automatic rifles in the hands of boys. In my Walter Mitty's world, it all worked out well for the tribes. Unfortunately, in the real world, they were denied access, and nothing good was decided upon. Life went on.

Brazilian Kayapo tribal chief Raoni and a bus carrying indigenous people and supporters was stopped outside the site of the Earth Summit yesterday after being refused permission to deliver protest notes. With him is rainforest preservation activist Lawrence Bishop. The disk in Raoni's lip symbolizes his rank as chief.

His picture was taken on the bus, at the gates, with Chief Raoni of the Kayapo (Caipo) tribe. I still have the clipping from a major newspaper, bird feather crown, porcupine chest plates, lip platters and all. CNN interviewed Lawrence about his perspective on the Earth Summit and asked about the indigenous people's situation. He elaborated, and stressed the fact that the people of the USA were so enamored with the movie *Dances with Wolves*. Here, in

South America, he said, we have a real life *Dances with Wolves* happening before our eyes. He asked, "Is anything going to be done about it?" That was his question for the world's inhabitants.

Next, he flew to Iquitos, Peru with his newly acquired Brazilian girlfriend, visiting and camping overnight on his newly purchased land. Then he signed the purchase agreement (written in Spanish, and Lawrence didn't speak, read, or write Spanish, DUH) and flew home. This is where my story begins, with *THE CALL*. You didn't really think I could pass on this dream of a lifetime adventure, did you?

Norman and Larry reunite, 1992

So, as you might have imagined, I decided to accept "Mission (almost) Impossible." We were talking about entering a foreign South American country, where the infamous *Sendero Luminoso* (The Shining Path, killers of 25,000 people) were still very much at large, and a total coup of the old (corrupt) government had taken place, organized by the new president. We didn't speak Spanish, knew no one, and were going to build a touristic eco lodge, 110 miles by boat from the nearest quasi-civilization.

I should have at least thought about it...you think? You know though, "Ya' snooze, ya' lose."

The preparation for the Peruvian project was what you might call a bit arduous. We sat for hours, days, weeks, almost a month, actually, on the Island of Kauai, through Hurricane Iniki's 200 mile per hour winds, with no electricity, food, or water in the house, trying to figure out every little problem that we could foresee happening. In the long run we failed, but we did deter countless obstacles.

UPSIDE

Lawrence had to go to Maui to phone in the $60,000 tool catalogue order that we put together (there were no services in Kauai for thirty days after the hurricane). There was one upside though: showering in a waterfall.

We did complete the task, and I did leave for Florida for final preparation and last-minute American purchases. We made plans for a meeting in Miami in two to three weeks. We were booked, flying to Iquitos, Peru via Rio de Janeiro in three weeks. (Lawrence wanted to see his Brazilian girlfriend and find a girl to occupy my time since we were going to be there for a full week.)

Back in Florida, it was the first week of October and the weather had improved, slightly. My mother appeared to be a lot less ill. It's really amazing what a bit of family energy can do for a busy but lonely person. (My mother was an incredibly prolific award-winning poet who never published a book. After this, my next book to publish and make available on Amazon will be a book of *Award-Winning Poems* by Kate Walters. I'm pre-pushing the book in hopes that you will buy or download it too, lol.)

My mission was to buy all of the necessary clothing, specialty tools, hot water shower bags, flashlights (there was no LED then, believe it), and whatever else I could think of, maybe a bunch of snacks. I spent a buttload of money, but I was able to spend some quality time with my mom, niece, and various extended family members. I spoke with my estranged teenage kids only by telephone, but I would be back for Christmas, and I had airline tickets for them so they could fly to Florida. I was reaching the actual spout of the funnel, and events were moving rapidly.

I had to pack all that I had purchased and deliver it to the freight forwarders in Miami. These guys were forwarding more than $75,000 worth of tools, solar supplies, and various sundry accessories to Peru for us. Their plane to Peru was like the shuttle to the space station—a complete necessity. Without this stuff we would be in the Stone Age, or the Bronze Age, or the S.O.L. Age.

- PART II -
INDIANA TO NYC

1969

CHAPTER TWO

Our first great adventure together was a lot like this one, except the tables were turned. Larry had just graduated high school, just turned eighteen, and had an adventurous spirit. I was twenty-one and had a plan. I had been playing in an acid rock band, White Magick, for about a year, and we thought we had material good enough to record. So why not go for the gold?

I had a good apartment in Goshen, Indiana, "The Land of Milk and Honey," we had a little money, we were young, and it was the summer of '69. So...I let a motorcycle gang, Sin's Slaves, stay in my apartment, which I then lost, because they rebuilt a motorcycle in the living room (the landlord didn't like that, and took possession of all my stuff). Hey, you live and you learn.

The guitarist (Jay), Larry and I, took off for LA with a short detour through New York City. At this point, it's probably a good idea to explain why we were going through NYC, from Indiana, to get to LA.

It was a real roundabout way, I know, but I had been casually walking around Goshen with a girl I was very interested in. She was artistic, intelligent, young, a real pleasure to talk with, and beautiful. She and her twin brother were visiting their older brother in the city, and I didn't want to pass up the opportunity to see her in a different setting. New York City in the sixties...can you blame me? Later, I'll hip you to how it all worked out.

In a borrowed 1952 Chevy with no hood and a tin can for an air filter, we made it into eastern Ohio. Then the engine blew. I grabbed my license plate and left the car in a turnout. I figured somebody could make a few bucks on it as scrap. I guess I thought we were going to drive that clunker all over the country. It ran fine in Goshen. It must have had an oil leak, or something.

This was our first taste of long-distance hitchhiking. Reaching a town in Pennsylvania where some of Larry's relatives lived took a while. They were very open-minded, or maybe just nice, and we had a good meal, sleep, and the next day we took a bus to NYC, courtesy of Larry's uncle. Last of the good guys.

Pulling into Grand Central Station in the early morning, not a cent in our pockets, was a bit intimidating to us country boys. When we pulled out our guitars and began playing, everything changed. Within the time it took to play one song, our favorite original composition, "I Love a Parade," there were twenty people around us, obviously grooving to our music.

I told the guys, "Be careful, and watch your stuff." Just the opposite. The onlookers wanted to give us money. Larry walked around with his hat, and for an hour we played songs to a revolving crowd. What a venue, GCS. We had no idea where we were going or how to get there, but we had enough money that we could eat and have fun. I asked around and learned that Central Park was happening, and so was Washington Square Park at the edge of the Villages.

Since we were looking for our friend near the East Village, we decided to go to Washington Square first — dead center, in the middle of the action.

Walking through the monolithic arch into the park was like

walking through the pearly gates. Greenwich Village on the right, and East Village on the left.

The park was a knockout. Nowadays it is beautiful, but in '69 it was crackling with kinetic energy. It seemed like anything one could imagine was there.

Washington Square entrance

Our friend John had moved to NYC a few months earlier and was living on 13th Street above the East Village. I got Larry to ask around and see if he could get directions to John's apartment. He came back and said, "John lives in the East Village, not far from here, but it's a little dangerous." We ambled uptown a few blocks and found his building.

The kicker to this whole drama was that John's younger brother and sister, twins, Bob and Bonnie (I mentioned her earlier, my reason for being there) had come to the city about a week before. They were being cool and getting an education, piggy-backed on. We were all friends, we knew they were there, they knew we were coming, and we were all going to use John's apartment as our base of operations.

We tackled the dark stairs, knocked on the distressed door, heard a few locks disengaging, and there they were. We had a great reunion with all three of them. We told of our odyssey, and they told of theirs. John explained what it was like to live close to the villages and his work.

We decided to take a little walk to Washington Square and play some music. The three of them were to meet us a little later.

John on 13th Street, NYC, 1969

There was nobody playing around the square at the time, so we pulled out our guitars. I plugged in and off we went on our magical, musical journey.

As we were singing, I saw Mike Bloomfield (The Blues Project guitarist) walk by, looking and listening but not stopping. Later, John Sebastian (from The Lovin' Spoonful) did the same thing. We were definitely in the hub of the music scene.

While we were taking a short break, a guy (a face in the crowd) straight out of *The Fabulous Furry Freak Brothers* (underground comics) came up to me and said, "Hey, man, you guys want to crash at my pad tonight? I have some good refreshments."

We didn't think we could lose, and John's apartment was full, so we sang, "YES!" in three-part harmony.

The Furry Freak who approached us was Jim, and he lived only a few blocks away (1st or 2nd Street, between Avenues A and B). Now we were entering the real danger zone. We played a few more songs, packed up, and were walking around the park when we ran into our friends.

Jim thought it was just wonderful that we had friends in the city, and invited them to come up later. He told them where to come that night and I saw John's eyebrows go up. Wow, things were just sort of clicking into place. We made plans for them to come up in a few hours. We hung out a while, and then moseyed on over to Jim's pad. He lived in a large loft with major deadbolts, and a bar that fit in a hole in the floor so the door could not possibly be opened once the bar had been inserted. Wow! I guess there were a lot of junkies who wanted your stuff.

The big room, on the street side, had a couple of grimy couches and a large rug that looked all one color, but might have just been dirty. Being the typical "crash pad" that it was, sleeping bags were strewn around, there were a few disaster rooms off the main hall, a large cockroach-infested kitchen, and last but not least, a dirty bathroom. Hmm.

If you've never seen *The Freak Brothers* comic book that I referred to earlier, you would not know what Jim looked like worn-out dirty gym shoes, baggy soiled jeans, and a large, stretched out T-shirt that might have been a light color once. His full, ungroomed beard started low on his neck and ended high on his cheeks, and he had black-framed glasses and long, very curly (electric) dark hair. To see him was to love him...just kidding!

His girlfriend was a sight to see. Short, thin, pinched face with a pointed nose and beady eyes, short curly brown hair, dirty fingernails, and who knows what else was lurking below the surface?

The place didn't smell really bad, but there were odors. We had some water and talked a bit, and Jim pulled a bottle out of the couch and offered everyone a pill (there were also two Puerto Rican guys, friends of Jim's, hanging at the table). We had come from the Midwest, so we said thanks and popped them. Everyone did. It was around 8:00 at night, and I wondered when our friends would show up. We just sat around and everyone talked their stories.

Things slowly got stranger and stranger, and I noticed that

Jim's two friends were no longer at the table, or anywhere around. By 9:00, we were glued to the couches, listening to Jimi grinding his guitar over broken glass (I love chewing tinfoil), laughing and talking amongst ourselves, when there was a knock on the door.

Jim opened the door and in rushed John, Bonnie, and Bob, our friends from Goshen, breathing hard with panic on their faces. Bob explained that he had just been robbed on the stairs for the ten-dollar bill in his pocket, at knife-point with his own knife.

We were in no shape to deal with this type of information. I managed to get out the garbled word, "WHOOOOOOO?"

To me, everyone looked like they were underwater, kind of, changing shape and transforming into animal characters.

"Two Spanish guys," Bob said. He added, "They ran down the stairs with my knife."

He went into greater detail, describing the actual encounter, and I felt like I was watching a movie. I'm afraid they'd lost their desire to socialize that evening. Jim immediately told us not to go out and try to find the thieves. Very dangerous, soooo...

Needless to say, our evening plans didn't come off very well. We spent another half hour, more or less, talking, and then they packed it up and left. Everything would have been different if we hadn't taken that pill, I just know it. It was a very good opportunity to hang out with the girl I had come to NYC to see. You get what you get, and don't get upset.

Deeper into the trance we fell, while Jim and his girlfriend began a series of strange skits. It seemed like play acting? Remember that little witch in the old cartoon "Little Lulu"? Well, Jim's girlfriend turned into that little witch, and Jim a furry animal, and they started relating as mother and son. This was really weird, but somewhat entertaining for a while. I suddenly realized that it was all just for our benefit. Ego-trippers always need an audience.

When I could finally talk again, I suggested that we find a different form of distraction. Jim, as the ringmaster, had a great idea.

"Let's hit the street and take the subway uptown," he said. With a twinkle in his eye he added, "The trains are free for us tonight."

Whew-boy, this guy was delusional. He also told us that no one would harm us, for the world was changing. No more money, no more greed, and we were the chosen ones. Nothing would cost us money. His girlfriend begged off and bounded off somewhere.

Jim talked us into taking our guitars with us, on us, not in their cases. He was like the snake in *The Jungle Book*, and I was actually starting to listen to him. Scary.

We descended the same stairs on which Bob had just been robbed. The two Hispanic friends appeared and Jim led the way. Halfway down the stairs I heard the steps creaking, and Julio pulled a knife out of his pocket. The light glinted off the blade and I realized it was BOB'S KNIFE. That meant... Then I remembered Julio leaving, then the knocking at the door. Oh man, we were walking down the stairs with the robbers.

That was nothing, though. Later we learned that the two of them were "The Heavies" of the East Village. Well, if you are going to be walking around the barrio at three in the morning, it is better to be walking around with the "Boss."

We hit the street, and Jim asked if anyone was hungry. I was pretty looped but the smell of pizza (the New York favorite) was everywhere, and we all agreed, PIZZA. New York City does not sleep. People were on the prowl. All six of us had pizza and a drink. We played our guitars, standing in front of a sliding window shop, and people stopped to listen and dance. We had a good-sized crowd, and some were buying pizza and drinks. When I tried to pay, the proprietor shook his finger NO at me. What?

I started seeing Jim Dent in a different light, dancing around like the Pied Piper. We carried on, happy as larks and singing at the top of our lungs at 3:15 a.m. We had an entourage following, but one by one they dropped off. When we entered the subway, there were only the six of us again.

I was starting to understand what Jim meant when he said nobody would harm us.

– PART III –
MIAMI TO IQUITOS, PERU

1992

CHAPTER THREE

My old buddy was due to arrive in Miami in about three hours, and we were booked to depart for Rio at midnight. I bid adieu to Jupiter, Florida and my family members, and drove the loaded van down Interstate 95.

When I arrived at our future Miami office, I learned that Federico, a well-connected Peruvian and our new office manager, had not yet received my letter of recommendation, vouching for me, from the Peruvian Consulate in Miami. My ticket to Rio was not confirmed as of that moment, either. We were to fly out in about four hours. Federico assured me that it would be confirmed, and not to sweat it. OK. Lawrence and Federico were readying last-minute schedules, timelines, and biz. We coordinated our info, had a bite to eat, chitchatted a bit, and the three of us took off for the airport. I still did not have a ticket in hand, but Federico got us in line and we advanced to the counter. Ready to go back home in a worst-case scenario, I was pleasantly surprised when my name popped up in the computer. I looked at Federico, and he smiled knowingly, handing me the letter of recommendation. What a guy.

We checked in, surrendered our luggage, and with our boarding passes in hand, we skipped through security (nine years before 9/11 and TSA), and boarded the plane. We picked good seats. I was the aisle man, and Lawrence was the window man. Looking around, I realized that it would be two months before I set foot in Miami again. Little did I know at that moment, that in the next ten years I would only return to the USA five times for short visits.

***

Rio de Janeiro *is* all that it is cracked up to be, literally. Nice hotels, lots of girls; clubs, lots of girls; congested streets, lots of girls; and beautiful beaches, girls everywhere with no clothes on. I felt like I was being put on the spot. I couldn't rest my eyes anywhere without staring at a partially, or totally naked woman. My Lutheran upbringing colored me shocked. Don't get me wrong, I lived the Maui-hippy-naked beach scene. The only difference was va va voom! But we only had plans to be there for a week, so I could take it as long as we didn't go to the water's edge too often.

One afternoon I was on the beach at Ipanema, trying to endure the embarrassment. (Oh, by the way, my old buddy set me up with Vanda [the aunt of his girlfriend, Adriana], who spoke

Sidewalk, blending water motif

only Portuguese [surprise].) We'd walked the streets all morning, observing the architecture, weather, and drinking espresso coffee with toasted baguettes and butter. I really liked the sidewalk tile designs and sketched as many as I could. The most popular motif was the mixing colors of the rivers, which appeared in varying shades and snaky designs as sidewalks twisted and turned through the city.

Anyway, on the beach, our topless girls noticed a commotion approximately a half mile down the beach. They suggested we pack up and leave. We were history to that beach. About an hour or two later, Lawrence called my room and barked, "Turn on the news, Channel Ten."

A wave of shabbily dressed young men was overtaking the people on the beach. The men were knocking people to the ground, beating and robbing them. You can probably guess by now where this happened. That's right, just where we had been. The whole beautiful, golden, sandy beach had been overrun by the youth gangs from the *favelas* (Brazilian slums).

Later I found out that the police had captured some of the boys, and word had it at that time that they were taken to the public dump and shot. I am not saying that *is* what happened, but years later I did see on the news, while living in Iquitos, Peru, the police in Rio undeniably doing that deed. It shook the world...then it was forgotten.

***

One night, we had reservations at a dinner show club featuring dancing women in incredible costumes. G-strings, feathers, exaggerated makeup, and incredible bods. Anyway, we were all spiffed out, jazzed up, and ready to go. The girls were dressed to kill. We hopped in a cab, but about a block from the hotel entrance, blue and red flashing lights appeared behind us. *This ought to be interesting*, I thought. Obviously, the police had been lying in wait for just this opportunity. $$$$$$$$. Everyone was checked, lightly frisked, everything out of pockets...the whole routine. I think they were looking for drugs. We were OK, but they needed $100 before we could drive away. There you go! There we went!

The show was outta sight, to say the least. Dinner was OK, and I fell asleep. That's normal for me. I've been known to fall asleep on stage, performing with a band. It's just who I am. Girls were great, drinks were watered down, we stayed too late and the taxi ride was uneventful, except for the B.J.s in the back seat. Just kidding! Or am I, my memory is kind of fuzzy.

We actually did survive all the room service, TLC, Jacuzzis, and massages, and I tried to fit in with the very different lifestyle I was encountering. After watching Christo (Jesus) on the jutting mountain, arms out, blessing the city, experiencing Copa Cabana, the girls from Ipanema, antique architecture, toplessness, thongs, and all the other boring stuff you encounter while in Rio, we bid our two girls a, "See you soon." They were going to be joining us at the new lodge in about a month, so we boarded the plane.

Yeah, that's right, we had four weeks to demolish the existing run-down buildings, and at the very least have some type of structures built to hide the beds. We could eat at the Dolphin Lodge, but it would be difficult sleeping there.

We flew out of Rio on October 23, 1992, my forty-fourth birthday (nothing auspicious about that). Of course, flying the Brazilian airline, Varig, we had to overnight in Manaus, North, and halfway between Rio and Iquitos, Peru. I spent a VERY uneventful night in the Brazilian Amazon Rainforest. One cool thing though, was the Santeria sacrifices and offerings along the roads to and from the hotel. Headless chickens and gutted animals, and always plenty of flowers and blood. Hey, welcome to the jungle!

CHAPTER FOUR

Iquitos, Peru, October 24, 1992. Touching down in a 737 jet on the cracked and broken runway, nestled in the middle of an incredible amount (a shitload actually) of trees, was a little unsettling, especially when we hit the ground, bouncing and slamming on the brakes. Larry and Norman were in the jungle again. A different jungle, but a lot of the same problems, I was sure.

Now, don't let me mislead you. Larry and I have survived countless life threatening situations, including freezing to death, drowning, hitchhiking across the US in the winter with our manly integrity intact upon arrival, being shot at by Hawaiians with M16s, ingesting very large quantities of experimental mind-altering substances (did we escape that one?), Woodstock, rock 'n' roll bands, the streets of lower east side Manhattan, three wives for me (I'm still with the fourth), and the list goes on and on, ad nauseam.

All that to say, this was not the end of days, and let me get back to what I was telling you about.

We were in the jungle for a specific reason: to create a new mode of adventure travel in South America: ecotourism. We would create a venue offered to those travelers who consciously believed it was important to try to live in harmony with their surroundings. Of course, it would also be offered to those who just wanted to see the "Lungs (or Jugs) of the World," and the animals, like elephants and giraffes. Whoops, wrong jungle (some people actually asked us about that).

Lawrence had been planning and scheming for this Peruvian adventure for a year or so, but I was green to the project (no pun intended), new to this jungle, and new to this quaint little 400,000 peep jungle town. I signed on to help engineer, construct, facilitate, mediate, and be, ultimately, the rubber on the road, go-to guy for the project.

Deplaning, I was assaulted by a wet blanket blast of thick, hot jungle air. Boy, I'd lived in the jungles of Hawaii, Thailand, and India, grew up with the muggy Indiana summers, suffered through the insect-infested months in Florida, but starting on day one, I learned a whole new respect for the word *SWEAT*! By the time I reached the open-air terminal, my shirt was soaked and stuck to my back. The sun was hot too.

Waiting with open arms was the Dolphin Lady, self-proclaimed naturalist/pink river dolphin protector, peddler of jungle land and fallen down lodges. Greetings all around, and I think I even saw L kiss her on the lips...OK. Young Peruvian boys were playing "El Condor Pasa," complete with panpipes (was that Zamfir skulking around in the shadows?) and young girls dressed in native vestments performing local dances, not lap dances. We struggled through baggage claim, immigration, customs, passport stamps, and then we were talking about the flight, the girls, and how we'd done in Brazil. I knew it was very interesting to the DL, but...

"LET'S JUST GET TO THE FRICKING HOTEL," I said. "Please?"

This had been a learning experience at every turn. Now we got to study: "How taxi cabs work in the jungle." The preferred way to get around, if your party was no more than two adults and three or four children (but this has to include a baby on the tit), is by small, two-cycle scooters.

I was accustomed to that from Southeast Asia, but I was very impressed by how well these people maneuvered on congested streets. A three-wheeled carriage-type motorcycle, called Motocar, the local term, was also common.

But wait, why did this 1965 Ford Galaxy 500 in front of us with no lights, no side windows, three colors, dented, and smoking, have its trunk open? Oh, it was our taxi. Hallelujah! I was dubious, but it got us through the twenty-minute obstacle course to the hotel, and actually drove away. Hallelujah again! The driver was Willy, who looked like Saddam Hussein and drove like Evil Knievel. We got to know him very well and even trusted him in the coming years.

We finally arrived at the three-star hotel, Acosta Dos, at around 3:30 in the afternoon. Not bad… There was a pool, clean rooms, hot water, and it was centrally located. My room was on the third floor. Exiting the elevator, yes there was a working elevator, I noticed there was a central atrium, ascending, first-floor pool, to the roof. I could dive into the pool when I left my room. No need for elevator or stairs (I remember thinking, *Watch your alcohol consumption tonight*).

I thought I better talk to the cute receptionist about moving to the first floor, then I wouldn't have to take the chance of bumping my head on the bottom of the pool.

My room was nice, queen bed, TV, and a large bathroom. I pulled the drapes and stood in awe, staring at the view. Miles and miles of rusted corrugated roofing. I think I even took a picture to send home.

I closed the drapes and left the room to meet Lawrence and my fate. Lawrence wasn't in the lobby when I arrived, so I decided to chat a bit in English with the cute, curly haired receptionist. That did help.

CHAPTER FIVE

When Lawrence arrived, he sort of looked at me out of the corner of his eye and went through the glass doors to the street. OK, I knew the girls were coming in a few weeks, and mine was the aunt of his girlfriend, but after all, I was single, not attached, and in a foreign country. Give me a break. And really, after all, I was kind of uncomfortable with the situation I was in. It was the first time in my life I'd had the opportunity to spend intimate time with a woman I'd just met, and one who led a very different style of life than myself. I'd work it all out, you betcha!

I hailed a Motocar (everyone called them that), and we took off, looking for a restaurant known as Ari's Burger. Can't go wrong with that (unless you are Hindu).

Traffic in Iquitos was relatively easy to understand. You had a very large river on one whole side, and mostly one-way streets, running to and from the river and up and down, parallel to the river. I just had to get the names of the streets in my noggin.

Iquitos is not accessible by land from other parts of Peru, Ecuador, Columbia, or Brazil, only by air, water, or hoofing it. I know there was a prophesy book that was popular a bunch of years ago in which the author indicated they drove to Iquitos from one of the outlying provinces. I guess that is artistic license, but not plausible in real life. Iquitos is an island, alone in an immense, swirling sea of green...trees. Its excessive population is misleading, for it has a small-town mentality. Most of the people know, know of, know about, or are related to everyone else. I am probably exaggerating, but let's call it artistic license.

Streaking down the main drag, through the madding crowds in the street and on the sidewalks, Latin beat bubbled over the sounds of bad mufflers and screeching tires. There were hole-in-the-wall eateries, mini-markets, street venders, appliance and TV sales (every block), boat and motor sales, and the Plaza de Armas. Every town has this plaza, or town square park. It is for the fallen soldiers from the many wars defending their country. People gather at the plaza every night. It is festive, with popcorn and snow cone venders, toys to buy for the kids (a million blown-up balloon toys of SpongeBob, Hello Kitty, Spider-Man and Mickey), a lit water fountain, and various other things. There are always girls, trolling with tantalizing bait.

Directly across Prospero Street (the main drag), riverside, was Ari's Burger, the fast, safe place to eat. It was like an oasis. We pulled up, got out, and paid the Motocar driver. This place was really something. Black-and-white checkerboard floor, red tables and chairs, twenty ceiling fans whirling away in this full, open-air corner restaurant. We ambled on over and sat down at a table, noticing that the waitresses were all uniformed up in short red skirts, tight white blouses, and red '50s diner hats on top. Yeah, baby! But who came to wait on us? A skinny, shifty-eyed, toothless man named Juan.

I said to L, "Is this a joke? Are we on *Candid Camera*?"

Juan spoke perfect English (a very good deal), it was just that we were expecting one of those *chicas lindas* to be tending to us. The ten-page menu, with photos, was in Spanish and passable English, proof that there was an English-speaking person involved. Was it

Juan? At least we didn't have to gringo bumble through ordering a late lunch. The menu was incredible, and I ordered an Amazon Plate, which offered a large fillet of grilled *paiche* (a local fish), rice, *chonta* salad (heart of palm leaf) with lemon juice and oil dressing, *yuca frita* (this is like French fries, but from *manioc* instead of potato), and three different local sauces, all *picante*. Oh yeah, and a local beer or two.

"Hey, how can ya go wrong?" I mumbled.

Juan said, "You can't go wrong. It is our most popular dish." Two points for Juan.

Lawrence eats differently than I do, and he ordered three different meals to make sure he got something he wanted. Great idea, because I could try some other things too, for ordering later. As we waited, I looked around at the clientele, waitresses, cooks, and finally the street. There were children of all ages selling jewelry, gum, shoe shines, jewelry, monkeys, cigarettes, crackers and chips, roasted peanuts, Indian fabrics, beads, more jewelry, and some very unsavory treats, I am sure.

There was obvious poverty, soiled clothing, bloated bellies, scruffy/dirty hair, mongrel dogs, but there was something else. Watching their personal interactions, I saw laughter and a look of strength and vitality in their eyes that was more "soul" than physical. The kind of thing we do not see in our country. Survival, maybe?

Juan asked if he could sit down and we accepted him. We were in the heat of explaining where we were from and why we were in Iquitos when I asked him, "Where did you learn to speak English so well?"

This question unleashed an incredible story that actually endeared this man to us for years.

Juan was born and raised in Iquitos. His father was one of the wheels of the local government. He told us that he was always an energetic hustler, and when he was in his early twenties he hitchhiked to the USA. Yes, South America is attached to Central America by a thin piece of gristle called Panama, and Central America is connected to North America the normal way. This was probably in the 1970s. People still hitched rides then, and caught them. We were still a naïve nation before the known "weird shit" started happening. Anyway, he made it all the way to New York State and settled in a small town in the north.

He finished learning English, worked, married, had a baby girl, and lived there for ten or eleven years. Then his life went south on him, and he did too. Back to Peru, hitchhiking. I believe he came back to Iquitos because of the tourism and family. His English was very good—he even knew all the slang and he could cuss well, too. That's a winning LOTTERY ticket.

He did OK, married again, had a ton of kids, and just painted himself into a corner. So, here he was in Iquitos, tied down, a guide, spoke English, and when he couldn't hustle tourists, he worked at Ari's Burger, hustling tourists. He made ends meet, because suckers came around all day, every day.

The food came and it was served well, looked delicious, tasted even better, and we ate to our hearts' delight because the servings were humongous. I'll describe the homemade sauces later. They deserve a time of their own.

We finished, kicked back, and asked Juan for the strongest coffee they had. He said that he would make it special for us. I didn't know what he meant, but was pleased with the outcome. I guess espresso did not exist in Iquitos, so he made us a concoction.

Lawrence and I sat and made plans over this thick, dark (excellent) java. He lit up a Dunhill. Me? Hand-rolled. I'd decided to smoke a bit on this trip, having taken a ten-year hiatus from the nastiness. I hand-rolled mine with Captain Black, mixed Cavendish, pipe tobacco, all nestled in a Rizla Black Licorice cigarette paper. Thick, rich smoke, with a luscious scent of exotic eastern spices and vanilla. An artist friend wrote a poem about my hand-rolled cigarettes once, dated 1968:

> *Attempting,*
>   *In a sophist way,*
> *Miming mouths sucking breasts,*
>   *Detached,*
>   *Elongated,*
>   *Rolled up,*
>   *Hairy,*
> *Black cigarettes.*

After a few weeks in Iquitos, all the shopkeepers, girls, street kids, and associates knew where I was, or where I'd been, by the "heavenly" scent. I didn't realize this until someone brought it to my attention, but by then it really didn't matter to me.

So, we had our first meal in Peru at Ari's and met the self-proclaimed "best guide" in Iquitos, all in one day. I was beat and wanted to head back to the hotel, but Juan came to the table and asked if we wanted to meet some girls. We had a big day planned for tomorrow, so I headed back. Last I saw of my old buddy he was getting up from the table and leaving with Juan. Uh-oh!

When I walked into the lobby of the hotel, I said hi to the receptionist and considered a swim, or was I tired? I thought maybe I'd just draw some of my thoughts from the day. Goodnight.

CHAPTER SIX

Over breakfast at Ari's (dinner was so good, we had to try breakfast), we charted out our day. First on the list was buying a boat and motor. Dolphin Lady joined us and introduced us to her breakfast companion, Rolan, our interpreter. She had lined up people she knew, or people who knew people she knew, to work for the new gringos. We would meet them one by one as we moved on, and most of them would crash and burn.

Now, Rolan was much different than Juan. He was low-key, a professional interpreter, English teacher, family man, and I think, an evangelist, so he wasn't going to be setting my old buddy up with girls (or maybe he would, money is money). What I started learning from the get-go, was there were no constants and there was no logic in the jungle. The shifting sands of the Amazon. Where did all this sand come from, anyway?

There are actual sand dunes all around Iquitos. You don't think that maybe, in one of the earth's plate shifts or continental movements, the Amazon River flowed the other way? That would explain the beautiful white sand and the shark sightings 2,500 miles from the Atlantic Ocean. Or maybe, the Amazon River cut South America into two continents, and the Pacific and the Atlantic Oceans were connected? I'm sort of getting off track here. Where was I?

Boats...motors...gotta buy one.

The four of us moved to the street, and lo and behold, there was Willy and his Ford. I now understood that Willy would be our driver, when needed. We piled into the heap, and because the DL (Dolphin Lady) was busy, we dropped her off and continued on to the river warehouse area where we were introduced to Manuel.

I noticed that Lawrence was sort of eyeing Manuel. L said to me, "I think that is the guy who sold me the land."

Small world? Or not. Well, Manuel also sold refurbished boats. He had three boats ready to sell to us. The first boat was fiberglass, a cabin cruiser, quite large, with an inboard motor. It was in relatively good shape. The second boat was aluminum, open, with a small motor, and quite obviously "Made in Iquitos." Last but not least, the third boat was a twenty-five-plus-year-old riveted aluminum Starcraft, which Lawrence or I had probably even worked on in Goshen, Indiana at our "summer jobs," which included shoveling out sheep sheds in the spring.

Oh, she was sleek, with the open gallery bow, covered cabin area, open stern, with an old 100 HP Johnson outboard motor (not looking good) that Manuel assured us was tip-top. Freshly painted with a new Naugahyde *toldo*, freshly re-upholstered seats, and new slatted floorboards, it brought back memories. What a beauty.

Let's take her for a spin!

Whoooaaaaah, cowboy, not that easy! Manuel's driver, Osvaldo, had to bring it through the swamp trails to a river club called Club Casa y Pesca, or The Hunting and Fishing Club. This was about an hour-long operation.

We met at the club on the bank of the Nanay River, which emptied into the Amazon River below Iquitos. It was almost as if it was all planned, because waiting for us was our next new employee, Melanio, boat captain, also called *piloto* or pilot. We all loaded up, Lawrence, myself, Rolan, Manuel, and of course, Melanio. Osvaldo stayed with his boat.

The Nanay is a black-water river and the Amazon is a muddy river, and when they meet, it's *café con leche*, or coffee with cream, a beautiful swirling tangle of waters, just like the sidewalks in Rio and Iquitos.

The motor sounded old, and I made that point to Manuel through Rolan. He assured me that it was guaranteed. That made me feel better. We were pretty happy, wind in our hair, sun on the water, and Melanio was an excellent piloto.

The old Starcraft cut the water like a knife and planed nicely. I believe we had made up our minds, Lawrence and I. We looked at each other and nodded. *We will buy this boat.* In a few days we were scheduled to leave port at noon for our first trip up the Río Amazonas. Off to our new home, the Río Yarapa.

– PART IV –
UNSUNG HEROES

Iquitos to the Río Yarapa

CHAPTER SEVEN

The Río Yarapa is the first feeding tributary into the Río Amazonas (the most powerful river in the world), after the confluence of the rivers Ucayali and Maranon. This is known as the "headwaters of the Amazon." (I will explain later where the Amazon River really starts. I had a spiel about that for the tourists.) We did purchase the boat, we christened it, and had the name **YACURUNA** and the registration number painted on its sides. *Yacuruna* is Quechua (the dialect of the Incas) for "Father of the Water." I guess we were a little full of ourselves, but it would be proven, in the not too distant future, that it was a very appropriate name. The club let us moor the boat there for a while, even though we were not members. We were riding on air and bullshit.

We had a few more business issues to address before leaving, but we were hungry. Ari's? Yeah, baby. I learned quickly that all the food not eaten could be given to the kids on the street. That was good, but sitting there watching five or more little ones waiting for food didn't quite make it for me.

I talked to Juan, and he asked the owner, Ari, if I could use one of his tables to buy the "Burger, Fries, and Drink Deal" for all the little kids who were around. The administration didn't like it too much at first because the kids were riffraff to them. They got used to it though. Money is money. The most I ever fed was eleven, three at a time, eating at the table. It cost me about $14.00. Sometimes there were only four or five kids.

I got to know all the kids, disabled people, and old women of the streets. I was in Peru for ten years, and those kids grew into teenagers and young adults whom I still know, see, and talk with every time I return. It's been twenty-five years now. Those who are still alive are adults, some with families, some entrepreneurs, some still in the streets.

***

Departure day arrived. We had introduced ourselves to Iquitos, gotten to know her somewhat, and now it was time to load up and shove off. The plan, we learned, was to travel up river in tandem with DL's boat, Osvaldo piloting. She had invited a few people — those important to the support of her project — to spend a few days at her lodge, have meetings, and hear what the new gringo boys had up their sleeves. Her guest list included one of the (Peruvian) president's top men and his wife (remember, there had just been a shutdown of the government due to corruption). This man's job was to assess the judicial arm of each province's local government, distinguish the good, the bad, and the ugly, and deal with it.

In the thirty days he spent in our district, we were able to get to know him and actually build a lasting relationship with him and his wife. Quite a few people got the boot in those days, including judges, prosecutors, and courthouse administrators.

DL had also invited a representative and two helpers from the *Ministerio de Agricultura*, or Department of Agriculture, who proved to be very beneficial later on.

We had three new employees, a chef, a construction foreman,

and an operational supervisor. All together we had thirteen people, two large baskets plus two boxes of food, drinking water, luggage, chickens (alive and squawking), some construction materials, two large coolers of ice and fish, and surveying equipment, all in two speedboats. No problem, right?

Everyone was at the dock and waiting. Luckily, the president's rep spoke great English and was from Lima, so we were able to distract ourselves with conversation. The DL (we soon found out she was always late) arrived at 3:30. This was not a good thing. We would be arriving at the lodge after dark, and that gave us no time for a "fudge factor." If anything went wrong, we would really be in the dark. Another one of our voyages into the unknown.

The Amazon River is an amazing phenomenon, miles wide in some places, strewn with islands, and tree trunks (bigger than cars) floating down river at more than ten knots per hour. On this particular day the river was like glass, and the first half hour of our maiden voyage was smooth as silk. This being our first trip, everything around us was strange. I kept my eyes and ears open.

We were about twenty minutes from the first pueblo, Tamshiyacu (named after a thin vine everyone used for lashing in the con-

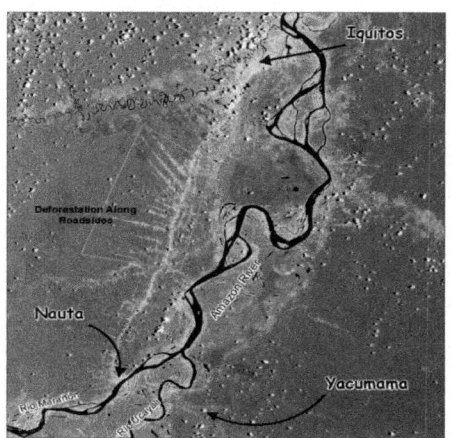

struction of their Maloka-style houses), when the motor on our boat started making strange sounds. I looked at our pilot, Melanio, and pointed aft to the motor. Melanio, with a worried look, nodded and pointed fore. I understood that to mean we would check it out at the floating dock at Tamshiyacu.

We pulled into the marina none too soon. The motor was wheezing and steaming, a real sick puppy. Lawrence went into the thatch-roofed outpost to buy mineral water and sodas for our guys, while I stayed with the boat to see what was wrong. Through Rolan, I learned that the head of the motor was probably cracked and the water was entering the housing. The real kicker was that *Yacuruna* could not go on. It had to limp back to Iquitos with whatever we couldn't stuff into the Dolphin Lady's boat...and her speedboat was two feet shorter than ours.

Well, we had always been survivors, the Great Spirit only knows how, so we decided to push on, forever onward and upward!

We loaded what we could into the dolphin boat, transferred some unneeded cargo into *Yacuruna*, and huddled to decide who needed to go now, and who could come on a river bus from Iquitos the next day. The DL's boat was overloaded, going to be slow, and was way past being dangerous. We sent Melanio off to Iquitos with all the excess weight and passengers, wheezing along a bit faster than idle. He'd be reaching Iquitos after dark. Losing forty-five more minutes to this drama was not in the plan, but off we went, under the threatening skies.

We had another translator for the journey (Rolan returned to Iquitos to act as our representative in this *Yacuruna* fiasco), our new operational supervisor, Esteban. (We found out he was really a guide, smart, and spoke English.)

An adventure is always exciting, like the unknown. We were on pins and needles with anticipation for about an hour.

"ARE THOSE THUNDERHEADS UP THERE?" I yelled, pointing to the sky ahead, trying to compete with the outboard motor.

Sure 'nuff, we were heading into a thundering rainstorm. I tapped Osvaldo, our pilot on the dolphin boat, on the shoulder and pointed to our oppressive enemy up ahead. He gave me a sidelong glance, scrunched up his lips, and pulled his finger across his throat...another uh-oh!

At this point I knew that we were going to get wet. The stuff that would get ruined in the storm was moved under the toldo, and since "earth suits" do not leak, people were in the open with rain ponchos. We sequestered the two women under the toldo. The rain began, not as sprinkles, but as sheets. Osvaldo looked back to me and made a gesture, like pulling a cork out of a bottle. I didn't understand at first, but then it hit me from past memories of building these boats.

There is a rubber thermos-type stopper in the stern of older boats, near the transom. When the boat is moving forward and taking on water (like in a RAINSTORM!), you can pull the plug and the water escapes by mere force.

OK. I was hunkering down about mid-ship, so I made my way aft. Waves were running diagonally against the hull, about a foot tall, with larger ones hitting us sporadically. Starboard (right-side) was weather side, and water was just starting to splash over the gunwales. My journey was only about five feet, but it was a rocky row to hoe. We were traveling into the wind, rain, and waves, so we had all the elements working against us.

I unsteadily reached the transom, stuck my arm down into the water — there was about a foot of it in the bilge — and surprise, I felt a small metal lever. I lifted it, releasing the tension, and pulled. I had the stopper in my hand. Mission complete. I looked forward, smiling, to Osvaldo, and held up the stopper just as a bigger wave hit the starboard side, sending a spray of water into the boat and knocking me off balance. Lawrence and two other people grabbed for me just as my leg hit the starboard gunwale. I would have gone over if Lawrence had not snagged my poncho. "There, but by the grace of God go I."

Rain was pelting the windshield, there was a chop on the river, the sun was going down, and we were headed into complete darkness. We all looked at one another, and I asked the DL if she had brought along spotlights.

"No," she said. "We never travel this late."

She had a weak battery flashlight, and we had at least an hour and a half, maybe more, of travel time (in the rain and darkness). Lawrence and I both had flashlights and I had some webbed rope in my bag. We donned another couple of ponchos, strapped flotation devices around our bodies backward, and climbed to the front of the boat, lashing ourselves to the chrome rails.

We were to be the Bearers of Light.

This boat did not have an open gallery in the front. We were actually on the bow of the boat, and we were very lucky that there were strips of wood running crosswise, meant for footing, to keep us from sliding off (in the nearly eighteen-inch waves). We were all deer in the headlights at this point, and you could smell the fear, sort of like "Teen Spirit."

My bubba and I were always up for a good laugh, so we just trudged ahead, knowing that there would be a great story to tell if we survived, and if we didn't, did it even matter? *Note: Hundreds of villagers are lost to the Amazon yearly. It is a recorded fact.*

The crashing of waves was merciless, we had our ponchos cinched around our faces, and our core body temperatures were dropping due to the rain and wind in the open elements. On and on we trudged, hour after hour, with the meager flashlights shedding enough light to avoid trees and debris. Where was that 1,000,000 candle power spotlight that I had bought? I'll tell you where. In all the stuff, at the freight forwarders, in Miami. Unhappy face emoji.

We were probably only traveling about twenty miles per hour, so I caught Osvaldo's attention through the windshield and made a palms-up gesture, pointing to my watch. He held up two fingers. Was that a "V" for victory? No, I realized he probably meant two hours, which was the answer to my palms up. Who needs words? Who needs translators? I was doing just fine, but only in that respect. Two more hours of this?

I noticed that Osvaldo had opened the snaps of the canvas boat top and had his head sticking through, I guess to see in the rain. There were a hundred little creeks emptying into the river (a mile across), waves, unmerciful rain, lightning and thunder, and no signs marking turnoffs (just to mention a few obstacles), yet Osvaldo was moving right along with eight people in his boat. A bit stressed, but not scared (so it seemed).

There was one moment when the rain and wind let up a bit. He motioned to replace the stopper in the bilge, then pulled into a creek turnoff, maybe just to rest. Within minutes, every inch of flesh that was not covered was occupied by sucking mosquitos — Amazon mosquitos. They *were* different. Everyone was wearing shorts. With everyone swatting, moaning, and jerking about, Osvaldo gave the signal to pull the stopper again. He gunned the motor and off we went, meeting the storm front head-on.

The passengers set sail that day, for a three-hour cruise, a three-hour cruise.

I could not keep that damn song from running over and over through my head. Fucking Gilligan and his three-hour cruise. The DL had told me that it was a three-and-a-half-hour trip, and trying desperately to check my watch, I saw that it had already become a five-hour trip (and counting). I caught Osvaldo's attention and pointed to my watch. He held up two fingers again. What was it with those two fingers? I would have been much happier with a shrug of the shoulders. Then I'd have known that we were all in the same boat (pun intended).

Sputter...cough...cough...sputter...cough...sputter...cough... DEAD IN THE WATER!

Well, that was quick. No beating around the bush, just dead, no sound. Osvaldo rushed to the stern and replaced the stopper. An oversight neglecting this small detail has sunk many a vessel. Somehow, the gas line from the portable tank had slipped out and was sucking air. He connected it again, yanked the rope two or three times, and off we went again, zig-zagging along, dodging logs and floating pieces of civilization. Minutes felt like hours, or maybe they were. We couldn't have been wetter, even if we had jumped into a pool.

It was really amazing that no one got sick on this ride. I guess fear takes priority. We were still holding the flashlights, teeth chattering, chilled to the bone, Lawrence giving me that zombie look, really not knowing how much more we could take. The rain was coming sideways at us, lightning flashing, thunder rolling across the sky, and...and...without warning, Osvaldo swung the boat to port and entered one of those small tributaries we'd been seeing for the whole trip, the Río Yarapa. Yeeeeeeee-haw!

Everything sort of changed, all of a sudden like. No big waves, no forceful wind, just regular rain and regular wind. Within two to three minutes, the rain started to let up and the wind died to almost nothing. Osvaldo slowed the boat, motioned for the stopper to be replaced, and I tapped my watch at him. He threw ten, twenty fingers at me and smiled. That was reassuring. A smile, and by the way, he smiled with his whole face and his heart. That was one fearless man (he knew how to handle a boat, too). We were through the worst of the storm, and in twenty minutes we would be at the camp.

Little did I know that in the next ten years I would take close to 500 trips up that river, and probably 200 of them would be in the pouring rain, with about twenty of those trips in conditions like those just described (but with a better boat, faster motor, spotlights, and experience under my belt).

No one can take the glory from Osvaldo. With what he had to work with, he faced each obstacle head-on and was never unsure of victory.

- PART V -
THE SUBWAY

East Village to Times Square
1992

CHAPTER EIGHT

We walked toward the underground subway entrance, six questionable men. Two with guitars slung from their necks, two Hispanic guys, Larry, and Jim Dent. We were more than just a motley crew, with our guitars, bell-bottoms, long hair, pinwheel eyes (hidden by dark glasses), and smiles from ear to ear, we were making history in NYC. I was edging more and more toward the seat on Jim Dent's bandwagon, especially when the subway police just passed us and nodded, smiling.

We came to the turnstiles, and here was where we would be turned away. Jay, the guitarist, and I lit up a tune, our favorite, "I Love a Parade." Now, I really don't know why that song was so popular. Everybody liked it. Possibly because it was so simple minded. I mean, the first line was,"I love a parade, see how many friends can be made."

It did have very nice harmony and a driving bass, and when it came time for the lead break, Jay tore it up. What more could you ask for? (I guess.)

Anyway, Jim was talking with the lady selling tokens. She was smiling and looking at us, actually enjoying the music and her night shift. All of a sudden she held out six tokens and dropped them in his hand. We entered through the turnstiles and got into the car. This is where it gets really weird at 3:30 a.m.

Who is on a subway car at that time in the morning? Homeless, misfits, thieves, maybe murderers, women of the night, men of the night, drunks, and people like us. We fit right in. We started at the very last car and worked our way to the front, singing and laughing all the way.

We had to change routes three times, but once you were in, you were in. We had a great hour of travel, waiting on the ramps, singing, and making a ton of new friends. There was no fear, no bad vibes, and no bad people. I guess that if there had been trouble, Julio and Manuel would have taken care of it. Great to know that someone has your back.

Emerging out on the street from the stark white lights of the subway station, I was shocked by the nightlife on Times Square. The street was still alive at 5:00 a.m. Everything was alive. We were alive. We didn't play much music there. It was so overpowering that we just took it all in. We walked around a bit and realized that we were becoming normal again. The spell was wearing off. It was time to return to our nest. I had to pay for the return trip, though. It was not like the first leg. We returned to Jim's apartment around six and crashed, hard.

***

I cracked an eyelid around midday and felt burnt around the edges. *What an incredibly magical (?) night, or was it a dream? Doesn't matter now*, I thought. I was in dire need of a shower, coffee, and food. I'm sure everyone was, but I was the only one up.

The shower was wet, and that is all I can say about that. There was no coffee, and forget the food. I rousted my mates, they showered, and we left.

"Shit, man. Should we try to connect with our Goshen

friends?" I wondered. I was feeling pretty bad about the night before, and wondering if they got back to John's apartment in one piece. I guessed that they probably had. We'd made it.

We headed back toward Washington Square, munched on a few pieces of pizza and walked west, toward Greenwich Village. Not much happening. I noticed a music store on the edge of Washington Square and we bought "handmade" guitar strings. Now, that was unique. Our thoughts were, *May as well change our old strings in the park...something to do, and then we can head up to Central Park.* Our coffer was getting low, but since we were there with new strings and a willing heart, we thought we might as well play some music.

A few hours later, we packed up and made our way uptown. Since we were in the "Square," we just took Fourth Street to Fifth Avenue and hung a left. We were only about seventy blocks away from Central Park, but Fifth Avenue gave us a chance to pull out our guitars and catch the lunch crowd—good money on the Fifth. Larry turned out to be an amazing "personal" manager. Jay and I would be playing, and Larry (in bell-bottoms, vest, no shirt, hair two different lengths from side to side, and hat in hand) would walk up to these people (three-piece suits and Chanel dresses), put his arm over their shoulders, and talk them out of money. They never acted put out, disgusted, or anything other than "happy."

I think I remember entering the Park around 72nd Street. We walked straight to the amphitheater. The Dead played there every Sunday when they were in town. Nothing going on, just people, people, and more people, and this was a weekday in early June. We walked over to the stairway leading down to the outdoor café and the Bethesda Fountain. This looked like a great place to play a few tunes.

Shit, man, we ended up playing for two hours, made a good bit of money, and then were invited to the café for a brunch with the "Beautiful People," and they were. One lady was very much into our music. She had long, flowing hair, a black leotard top, and the most amazing long white fringed deerskin pants that I had ever seen (and I had designed and made leather clothing for people in Elkhart, Indiana for a few years, yuk yuk).

This one, who introduced herself as Thayer, invited us to the café. We were living a dream. Artichoke appetizers with melted butter and fresh prepared mayonnaise, little toast things with caviar, and sangria. I wasn't a big drinker back then, but that sangria was good with all the sliced fruit floating around in it. When we were leaving the café to travel downtown (to Washington Square), our mystery lady mentioned there was a party she wanted us to play for.

She said our music was angelic. A far cry from acid rock, but I was playing a Höfner bass guitar (same brand and model that Paul played with the Beatles) with a powerful battery-powered amp. Jay, the guitarist, had a Gibson Hummingbird. I could imagine, with the harmonies and the tinkling music, that we could be angelic. OK, I liked that.

CHAPTER NINE

We played quite a few parties with this group of people. The first one was probably the most memorable for me—a twenty-nine-room palace on East End Avenue, near the Gracie Mansion. There was an art gallery filled with notable art, a music room where we set up and played, eleven bedrooms, ten bathrooms—you name it, they had it. Tons of large, overstuffed pillows cluttered the floors for lounging purposes. All the furniture was antique, all the floors were covered in Oriental rugs. Was this too much, or what? Last night in a flophouse in the East Village, with robbers wandering all night in the subway. Tonight on East End Avenue. Hmm, I've always loved juxtaposition; it was my favorite in art school.

Well, we did meet a bunch of people. The condo belonged to Bob and Marina, but the guests ranged from all the "DEAD," to artists and musicians, tons of trust fund kids, groupies, hangers-on, doctors, lawyers, models, newscasters, oh yeah, and a dentist—that is where the nitrous oxide came from. There was this one guy, Brucie Baby, who got his lip frozen to the tank. That was quite a trip, getting him free. Later, pizza was ordered and Brucie couldn't keep it in his hands, so he scooped it up off the Oriental rug and shoved it into his mouth. That was the high point of the night.

A few weeks later, at another party, Charley, a lawyer in the bunch, brought a visiting opera singer (Chilean or Argentinian, I just can't remember). She was quite famous and was singing that night at the Met. Brucie dosed her with a very large dose of Sunshine Acid. It was her first psychedelic experience, and needless to say, she didn't sing that evening. Everyone was pretty pissed at 'ol Brucie, but he was a real prankster and everyone knew it.

We just kinda' sat around and gawked at first. But you know, you get used to weirdom pretty quickly in NYC. Remember what I said about "last night and tonight"? East Village to East End Avenue. I just watched my mind being ping-ponged around. Nothing I could do. Nothing I wanted to do. Nothing I was able to do. But we sure had fun being the bumpkins from Indiana. Everybody loved us. Unfortunately, we were just about nine months late to really cash in on the help that "those" kinds of people (money people) give to "our" kinds of people (singer-songwriter-musicians).

It appeared that a group of music boys called the "Silver Dream" had come into their lives at that time. The money people backed them with apartment, money, recording time, a demo, and more money. Offered them fame and fortune, stuck with them, and were thrown under the bus when the boys decided to go to LA with a contract from an unknown studio. They were remembered as the "Aluminum Nightmare." Too bad, but we were doing OK. More or less. But listen, Thayer invited all three of us to stay in her apartment on 72nd Street. She was staying with a friend in a houseboat moored on Staten Island. We were making money at parties and on the street, reading for movie scripts, being referred to music producers and recording studios, and living a truly expanded life.

The pinnacle, I believe, was when a new friend, Cash (friends with Far-out Frankie, one of the crazy people we met in the parks), asked her ex-husband, a producer, who had a new band starting up, to come and listen to her friends in their apartment on 72nd Street. Not quite correct, but close enough.

Well, he came, a real "PRO," and listened to the music, vocals, arrangements, and said, "I really don't have the time to try to introduce a new group with your style of music, even though it is very good. But I do need a bass player, and you're really good. You have a refreshing new style, and I love the chords you slip in sometimes to augment a certain drama into the music."

And I said, "Why thank you." Stars in my eyes.

"Would you like to come upstate to try out with the group?"

UH-OH. My mind went into analysis function. Did I hear correctly that he only wanted me?

Then he went on to say that Jay, our guitarist, was, "Egotistically centered on his music, and very erratic."

Now, all these words rattle around in my brain from time to time, but the next words that I spoke will always nip at my Achilles' heel:

"No thanks," I said. "I have a group and we have a bright future. We are starting a demo next week."

He said, "Great, but if you change your mind in the next week, here is my card, give me a call."

WONDERFUL...NOT! The new group was THE BAND, famous for the album *Music from Big Pink*.

***

We had arrived in NYC in the first part of June. We played around and had an incredible time. We met and became acquaintances with many powerful people. It was the end of July and we were on a roll. Staying for just a few days, watching a new friend's penthouse on Park Avenue, was just too cool. We were on the fifth floor and this pad had an electrified glass skylight.

It was about 10:00 p.m., and Larry and I were just kicking back, looking at the stars, when Jay came in and offered us a large, ugly, speckled pill. I said, "Where'd you get these?"

We had been supplied with unlimited quantities of "ORANGE SUNSHINE" LSD for the last couple of weeks by the actual chemists—names not to be divulged (Google it)—and I wondered what he was doing, getting something from the streets.

"No, man," I said. "We are just kickin' back with the stars."

Jay looked at me and said, "Great, see you later," and popped two of the pills into his mouth.

I said, "What the hell you doing, man?"

He looked at me and said, "Gettin' high." He raised his eyebrows and walked into the other room.

OK. That was really a dangerous action. I followed him into the kitchen and said, "Man, you better barf those up."

He just looked at me, pulled out his guitar, and started playing a really nice, new riff. Great, I got my bass and started playing along. We always made good music together.

A half hour into our jam, I noticed that he started injecting strange notes into the chord progressions. It was not like him to do this. The music became a little bit dark and attracted the attention of Larry, who came into the kitchen and asked, "Hey guys, what's going on?"

I looked at him and just shrugged my shoulders. Jay looked at him with a Gollum-like expression, got up, put his guitar away, and left the penthouse. We didn't see Jay again for a year or more. The real kicker was that "The Band" had already signed a bass player. That poor camel's back was broken.

– PART VI –
BOATS AND MOTORS

Dolphin Camp, Río Yarapa
Back to Iquitos

CHAPTER TEN

Arriving at the Dolphin Camp, reeling from our river trip, I peeled my water-logged clothes from my shriveled body, showered in cold water (the shower bags were in Miami), changed into dry clothing, and ate a hot meal of chicken and rice, which had never tasted better. Accompanying this splendidly simple meal was *refresco de maracuya* (passion fruit juice made from fresh fruit), and our favorite, yuca frita (yoo-ka). Remember that? The French fries made from manioc.

There were those great sauces again! Here I go...

The first one, *cocona*, was sort of yellowish and watery looking (lime juice), with pieces of a fruit and a very tangy, salty/sour taste. My favorite of all time.

The second one, *salsa amarilla* (yellow sauce), was prepared with crushed *ají mirasol* (hot Peruvian yellow peppers), garlic, and fresh-made mayonnaise. Very good on the yuca frita.

The third one, *huacatay*, a Peruvian herb (related to the marigold and tarragon), crushed and mixed with lime juice, oil, mint, and garlic, was great on the chicken.

The fourth one, *salsa roja* (red sauce), was finely chopped *ají rocoto* (very hot Peruvian red pepper), mixed with garlic and lime juice. *Muy picante*.

See, I told you I was going to give them their due.

Sitting back after dinner, looking at all the survivors, I thought we looked pretty good. No shell shock that I could see. We all got to know one another a bit and dealt with the trauma of our ordeal by recounting it and laughing. We had all made it in one piece, amazing!

By this time it was going on 10:00 p.m. and I was falling asleep. Lawrence, who is a night owl, wanted to go over our plans for the next day. Not for me, too much input. I stumbled out to our bungalow, flashlight in hand, opened the door and looked around. Not bad, two single beds with mosquito nets, a shelf on each side, a table and two chairs and a snake. Whoa! Luckily, the snake was as surprised as I was, and it escaped through a large crack in the floorboards. I placed that experience in the front of my memories.

WARNING! Check floor!

Lying in the musty bed, trying to relax again, reality was getting a bit fuzzy when Lawrence walked in.

"Man, what a place," he said. "I can't wait until tomorrow. It'll be light and we can get out in the jungle. God, what a place."

"Yeah," I responded. "What a place!" Literally.

As the cool rain slid in long silent strings from the edge of the thatched roof, it caught the reflection of lightning in the southwestern sky. It was incredibly beautiful. Then the loud crack of thunder and rolling resonance carried the rhythm of the storm deep into the jungle. I was off to another reality.

***

Our first week on the river was to consist of exploring the land, meeting our crew, deciding on the lodge site, and making material and tool lists for Iquitos. Before we left for the Yarapa, we received news that our shipment from the US would not arrive for at least two weeks…bummer! That meant we had to postpone everything for two weeks or buy tools for thirty workers.

Was this a no-brainer? OK, that would mean hammers, saws, levels, squares, plumb bobs, nails and more nails, post hole diggers, shovels, rakes, machetes (no, these were not to protect us from the restless natives), and wood. Boy oh boy, were the *ferreterías* (hardware stores) going to love us.

Monday morning was truly a spectacular sight. You know, the kind of morning when you open your eyes, sun is filtering through the window, flooding the room with a warm yellow glow. Birds are singing, cocks are crowing, hens are clucking, and you can smell wood smoke mixed with jungle flowers on the cool morning breeze. Can you get better than that? How about fresh fried *piraña*, papaya slices in lime juice, thick sliced homemade bread toasted over the open fire coals and slathered with butter and jam. I was ready to start the day after that.

Pan-fried piraña

DREAM OF A LIFETIME

***

This was the moment of truth. We were really going to start this "project" in this moment, right now. Esteban, our "Operational Supervisor and Guide," came over to our table and introduced himself, again. He was our translator for the boat ride—a person you would see once and never forget. He was a very strong and proud native man. His skin was the color of mahogany, and his face looked as if it were sculpted from the same wood. Jet-black hair, a high forehead, prominent brow and cheek bones, flared nose and dark eyes, all made for quite an impression. If he painted his face (which he often did for tourists) and dressed traditionally, you would swear he had never seen a white face.

"Well, Esteban, what is the plan for today?" I asked.

"Mister Mormon, I—"

"No, Esteban, I am not a Mormon, I am Norman," I chuckled.

"Oh, I am very sorry, Mister Norman." He suppressed a smile.

Esteban's job for the week was to talk to the villagers and record the names of those who wanted to work; talk to people about materials; fix prices; and make plans for the next week. Then we would be ready to begin.

Esteban

Our plan for the week was to have a good time, explore, accustom ourselves to living in the jungle, get to know the guests, and work on a few craft projects. Very good planning. We did get to know a few of the local villagers who had the courage to approach us with trade items. They wanted money, and we wanted items that we could use to make a talisman, walking stick, cane, necklace, and any other type of

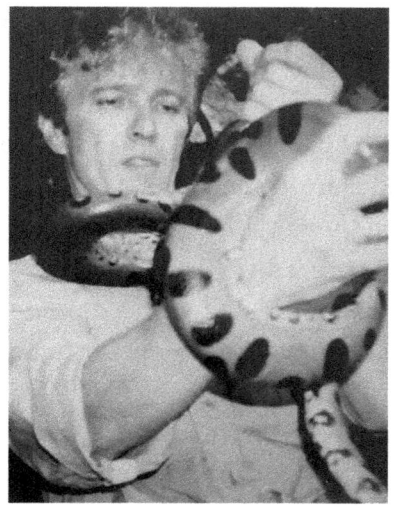adornment. It all worked out well and everyone was happy.

One man brought a boa constrictor up to trade. That was the last thing we wanted to start doing, and we told Esteban to advise the villagers that we were not in the market for animals or animal products. But...I bought the ten-foot boa, only because the man would have killed it or taken it elsewhere to sell. I think I paid ten dollars for it, and he was happy. After they were gone, I let it wrap around my arms, holding its head (of course, a bite from one of those snakes can give a very bad infection), and walked deeper into the jungle behind the camp. It was a youth, young and strong, just caught. I let it go with a prayer and wish for its well-being.

Through the week that ensued, we made our way through the jungle. There are two ways to build in the jungle. Cut everything down, build what you want, and let things grow up around the perimeter (the only drawback is, you have no shade from the Amazon sun). Or, only cut the saplings and the brush around the big trees, and still have habitat and plenty of shade. OK. No big trees cut. Our elevated walkways (insurance against poisonous snakes) actually snaked (pun intended) their way through the jungle, around the trees. The branches on these 150' trees didn't start until about fifty feet above the ground. No pruning needed. We did great, carving out our plan that we had developed in Hawaii. I'd say that we were able to stick with the actual drawings (especially since I'd never seen the place) with about 75 percent accuracy. Not bad, if I do say so myself.

Everyone thought we were nuts, even Esteban. It is so much easier to build and move materials if there is nothing in the way. But who wants easy?

Within this same week, the people who'd had to return to Iquitos (in the rainstorm) arrived and started their work: surveys, meetings with the Dolphin Lady, etc. The mayor of Iquitos, Jorge, also came out. We had a lot of fanfare preceding us, and I believe he wanted to know what our plans were. We had a few pleasant evenings with everyone and I played some of my songs for them. Everyone enjoyed themselves, even if some didn't understand.

La Arca

Lawrence had bought an old wooden excursion boat in Iquitos after the Earth Summit. Her name was *La Arca* (The Ark) and she was fully livable. Larry had given his authorization for the president's man, Raul (who came to the Yarapa with us, along with his wife), to use the boat in his absence to go up the Nanay River toward Ecuador for the purpose of investigating a huge oil spill. This spill, close to the border, was moving toward Iquitos. Well, the long and the short of the story is that it was a devastating spill. There were thousands of floating fish (big and small), and dead wildlife everywhere—kilometers and kilometers of rainbow water (the water all villagers needed for their families). Raul, his wife, and Jorge (the mayor), all spoke English. This made evenings a lot easier for us as the new kids on the block.

Raul took this trip with a complete crew sometime in the third quarter of the current year. He then had returned to Lima and suggested a very stiff fine (in the millions) for the oil company. Oil companies carry a lot of weight in Central and South America. They are almost untouchable, hard to kill, so I never heard the final outcome of this suit. I would not be surprised if they walked away with a slap on the hand.

While I was living and working in the jungle (much later), the nearby Pacaya-Samiria National Reserve (about four hours upriver) fell prey to the oil people (Texaco). They were drilling in the middle of the wilderness (the reserve protects 2,080,000 hectares, or 5,140,000 acres) where no one could keep an eye on them. They had a blowout and spill. The talk from the drunk roughnecks in Iquitos was that it was three times the size of the Valdez. It was stuffed and forgotten. No clean-up, no fines (that I ever heard of). They just went on drilling and pumping. Of course there were ugly tell-tale signs in the Río Maranon, like foamy sponge-like crap and thick, stringy rainbows on the surface of the river for at least a month.

The week went by very quickly, and we prepared for our trip downriver to Iquitos. We knew it was going to be a rigid weekend with all the plans we had sketched out.

***

The boat ride back to Iquitos was quite different than the boat ride to the Yarapa. As a matter of fact, it was so nice, cool, sunny, and windy, that we all (even Raul and his wife) napped on the way back. This was going to be a big weekend. We had to get *Yacuruna's* motor together, find and rent a huge boat (to haul 8,000 board feet of hardwood) and send it off to the Yarapa, and buy a bunch of tools for the guys in the jungle to use. Our plan was to get this all done and leave for the Yarapa by Monday or Tuesday.

In most Spanish-speaking countries, *siesta* (or midday lunch/

sleep) is from 12:00–3:00 p.m. Nothing moves. I learned quickly (with much frustration) that I needed to arrive in Iquitos, from the Yarapa, at around 2:00 p.m. That way I could get into the Hotel Acosta, eat at Ari's Burger, and be hitting the pavement when everything opened back up at 3:00 p.m. Everything, even the bank, was open until 6:00 or 7:00 p.m.

We hit the bank first. The transfer from the USA had arrived. We could pull a bunch of money out and accomplish something. We had opened our account the week before, and our checkbook was waiting for us. We could pay for the big bucks items with checks.

But this was not true. I thought rubber checks were out of control in the USA. Well, if you accepted a check here, you deserved what you got.

Our first line of attack was to get the *Yacuruna* moving. The motor was deemed "JUNK" by the local "new" motor dealer, COREPSA. Manuel gave us a $700 discount on the boat package, but guess what? We had to take the boat to COREPSA to install the new $6,000, 150 HP Fast Strike motor that we bought. Now here's the kicker: no one had a boat trailer to lend us that we could use to pick up the boat, ten miles away at the nearest dock. Manuel knew a man who had a trailer for sale though, for $2,500 (I was LMFAO at this point). We secured it for $2,000, rented someone's truck (to haul it), delivered the motorless boat Saturday morning, early. We were promised pick-up on Monday, motor installed. Number one, DONE.

Our second attack was the "Big Boat." We had to go to Belen (the floating city) to find one. It was one big-ass boat, about sixty-five feet long, had below-deck storage, and a flat metal roof to facilitate access to the latrine and motor (in the stern of the boat) when it was loaded with cargo. It was powered by a 100 HP Johnson (OH NO!) outboard motor. The captain said that it would take two days to arrive in the Yarapa because of the weight: 45,000 pounds or 22.5

tons. Number two, DONE. It was time to hose everything down, get something to eat, and get some sleep. Zzz.

***

After a well-deserved meal and sleep, we were ready to greet the day at Ari's. The best thing about breakfast at Ari's was everything. Atmosphere, girls, Juan's special coffee for us, food preparation, and Juan's explanations of the workings of Iquitos. We were mulling over the idea of using Juan for some exploration and discovery work in Iquitos. It seemed like he had the answers to every question we could voice. When we needed an item, he knew just where to get it. Hey, I thought, that might be a good thing for Juan to do: oversee the loading of the wood boat. It certainly would free us up to go buy the tools and materials.

That is what we did. Juan did a great job and made some good money for his eleven kids and his extended family. We just pointed him in the right direction. We even talked him into riding out to the lodge on the supply boat to guard our stuff. Later I'll tell you about his voyage to the Yarapa on the supply boat. "HAIRY!"

COREPSA had decided to work on our boat on Sunday, also. They wanted to finish the installation and have us pick it up on Monday. The mechanic, Octavio, and his assistants, would meet us when the boat was back in the water, sync everything, and test it out on the river.

We were getting excited now. I figured we might as well head off to Ari's for some coffee and a cig. I guess it was past lunch time. We thought we would just get a snack and eat at the hotel later. It certainly was different without Juan at Ari's. He was out working…for us. Lawrence and I had to use our sign language skills. It worked, kind of. It was a lot easier with Juan.

Damn, I started thinking some weird things about this time. Could Rolan be part of the DL's shell game? I know that she hooked him up with us. He seemed like such a nice guy, a little bit spiritless, but nice. But wait, he was the translator for Lawrence at the first deal. The land deal. Lawrence did not speak Spanish, could not have understood what he was signing, and Rolan had read it to him, translating as he went. Some day I would have to look into that. I didn't even have the sale document, Lawrence had it. I brushed it off, I'd ask him later — too much to think about.

One thing I did do, though, was to make a mental note: *Juan as my translator? My go-to guy?*

CHAPTER ELEVEN

Monday morning did come around, bright and early, and I was up and about and admiring the beautiful rusted roof panorama. I was on the second floor this time, and I do remember making a drawing of it with natural rust coloring. I was, and am still, always up before anyone else, so I ordered coffee from room service and settled back to think.

Let's see, the timeline, target date…

RINGGG…RINGG…

I answered the phone. "Hello?"

Lawrence inquired, "Hey, you up?"

"Is a bear Catholic? Does the Pope shit in the woods?" I replied.

He chuckled. "I'm in the hotel restaurant. Let's plan the day," he said.

"Got it, be there in a few."

Things were going well, knock on wood, ha ha ha. Now we had to find the wood. Guess who had a friend, who had a friend, who knew a place where we could buy wood? The Dolphin Lady, that's right. The first friend was Manuel, the second friend was the guy with the trailer, and the guy with the wood turned out to be a *new* member of their gang. We all went to view the wood. It was very nice—dry, straight, and stacked by length. I wanted the longest boards possible. In Peru, that is thirteen feet, but the most amazing thing was the various widths of the boards. Some were up to twenty-eight inches wide, and we had a very good species array. Rolan translated for us as we negotiated price, from the unheard of to the absurd. I was starting to think that Rolan knew more than he should. What could we do? We were strangers in a strange land. BEND OVER…hold your ankles.

We bought it, of course. Manuel said he would be in charge of making sure everything went well (for a price). "Sidebar please!" I was seeing a very clear pattern here. It seemed like everyone was scripted into their parts except for us (fresh meat). Remember that it was Manuel's land (?) the Dolphin Lady sold to Lawrence; Manuel's boat that we bought; and the guy with the trailer was the one who knew the wood guy. It was like someone was leaking all of our conversations to these people. They knew what we wanted before we even mentioned anything.

OH WELL!

Lawrence and I work well together. We have always accomplished a lot when bludgeoning a situation, and we had our translator, Rolan. We were actually able to do business. We understood, and they understood—the only way to roll. There was only one major hitch…our tools and equipment from the USA.

Lawrence and I went to the COMISA ferretería around the corner from the hotel. We met Roger, a young Chinese man, who would become one of my closest Peruvian business friends (still is today). Roger, son of the owner, and Santiago, who was known as "Santi," waited on us. The store had a very good feeling, and they had everything that we needed. We probably spent a good hour and a half looking and buying from every department: tools, lanterns, plumbing, building supplies and materials, ten-gallon gas containers, and 1,000-liter water tanks. This was a considerable amount of money, and they did not accept checks (we would have to get more money to take to the jungle for payroll and for serendipity). We decided to have everything delivered to the dock, and the supply boat could pick it up with Juan aboard.

Peru isn't like the US, where you can call a company and ask if everything is ready. In Peru, you really have to go to the location to talk directly to the manager, or mechanic, or whoever. (Also, cell phones were not available in 1992.) We did an amazing amount of running around in Motocars. Sometimes I felt like a dog chasing my imaginary tail.

We made our plan and took off for COREPSA.

The motor was installed, and I sent a runner to alert the truck owner that it was time to move the boat back to Nanay. We could not dock or float the boat near Iquitos because the banks of the river were thirty to fifty feet tall. That's right, the city was thirty feet above the Amazon River at that time of year.

We stood around for about an hour, admiring the new motor and talking to Rolan, waiting for the truck. When it did arrive, hook-up was relatively fast and funny (if you like the Three Stooges movies), and we were on our way, ten miles and thirty minutes. The mechanics assured me that they were following and would be there shortly.

About an hour later, the mechanics arrived, toolboxes in hand. It was getting to be about 9:30 a.m., and we were feeling the strain. We would have to be on the river in about thirty minutes to be able to leave Iquitos by noon. NOT. It took them about an hour and a half to get the motor running properly, and then we went out on the Río Nanay to test it (remember, it was the first all-electronic motor, sort of "Solid State"). It was only a 150 HP, but it really performed...until it died. They fiddled with this and fiddled with that, rewired this and unwired that. Finally they got it all synced and it was smooth as silk. We cut through the black water like a fish. Very impressive.

It was 11:45 a.m., and we had to journey a thirty-minute ride back to Iquitos, feed everyone, load the boat, and get our stuff from the hotel. We'd be on the Río Amazonas between 2:00 and 2:30 p.m. If we were lucky, we would be in the Yarapa by 5:00 p.m., max. I prayed that this was not a déjà vu moment.

When really bad, unexpected things happen, you believe that anything can happen, and never really trust anything to go completely as planned. Prepare yourself for the worst, and when things go well, you are surprised and happy, and when things go south, you are ready for them. "Once bitten, be twice shy." Well said.

Before we started out for the Yarapa, we had to deal with the "gold-plated" boat trailer. There was no place that we could store it, but Manuel had a deal for us. He'd store it for us if he could use it any time he needed it. Jeez, that was a deal we couldn't refuse. What else could we do? Give it away, drive it into the deep river? Shit, man. Our hands were tied.

"Manuel, that is the best deal I have heard today," I said.

"Deal done," was translated by Rolan!

CHAPTER TWELVE

We did make it out of Iquitos by 2:45 p.m. Our pilot, Melanio, assured us that he would have us at the lodge no later than 5:30 p.m. We made sure that the supply boat had left in the morning with all the stuff. This included 150 gallons of gasoline, fifty gallons of *petróleo* (diesel), and twenty five-gallon containers of drinking water. Juan was on the boat, for sure, and they had left port at 9:00 a.m. They were slated to be in the Yarapa by Tuesday night, more or less.

We all leaned back in the newly upholstered seats and relaxed, except Melanio, of course. He had his eyes peeled, looking at the surface of the river. There really are logs the size of trucks floating down the Río Amazonas at ten knots per hour. The real kicker is that there is only one inch of wood showing above the water. These pilots need to have eyes that are trained to identify and evaluate all data that enters their sight. Some decisions are split-second reactions. Now, he did have a few accidents in the years he drove for me, but the times he saved my ass and the boat outnumbered those.

It was a pretty mellow trip up the river—nice and glassy, smooth, and not a lot of debris. I was happy, burning these fifty gallons of gasoline up, and fifty gallons down. Outboards are not known to be fuel efficient, which is why everyone now has four-cycle outboards. Better gas mileage, and less contamination. We were 110 miles from civilization, traveling at forty to fifty miles per hour against a twelve-knot current. You do the math. I cry too easily.

It was only Lawrence, Rolan, myself, and Melanio on this trip. *Tranquilo*, as they say in Spanish. I looked over at my bubba, sleeping like a baby, and flashed back to that flophouse in NYC more than thirty years before. We'd been through a lot, survived more, and we were back at it again. Incredible. We pulled up to the dock at the Dolphin Camp at 5:45 in the late afternoon, right at dusk. We were sitting just four degrees south of the equator, and darkness fell right around 6:00 in the evening. The sun rose around 6:00 in the morning. It was easy to calculate one's schedule with a simple timetable.

A peaceful evening in the jungle. We brought the food on the boat and Misael, our new chef, jumped right in, cooking up a storm. We had a great meal of grilled dorado fish, grated wombok and carrot salad, rice, beans, fried plantains (chifles), and Mocambo juice. Afterward, a very cold beer. I think that they always prepared a lot of food for us because the employees got to eat all the leftovers. I finally put two and two together when all the full-time employees gained weight. I mean really. We did throw money and food around, I admit, but hey, spread the good around a bit. I guess this is true until it starts biting you in the ass, which it did.

I was beat, so it was time for me to turn in. I had patched the hole in our cabin floor — you remember the snake's door — so I felt a bit more secure. As I lay there in the dark, an orchestral cacophony of sound assaulted my ears until I relaxed enough to actually hear the sounds of the jungle. Lord, it was a symphony of sound, incredibly orchestrated. All the mating calls coming together created an overture called, "Gimme some lovin.'" As I was falling off into never-never land, I swear I heard the bass, the cello, violin, piccolo, oboe, and the marimba. What would the music be without the marimba? Nighty-night!

***

Oh boy, another beautiful morning in paradise, or is it paradox? I always slept well in the jungle, waking refreshed and ready to tackle the day. Sometimes, I really had to tackle the day. Coffee was always the first thing on my mind.

After another exotic breakfast of fresh fruits, toast, scrambled eggs, and fresh-squeezed juice, Lawrence and I decided to take another look at the old lodge up the not-so-lazy river. Melanio readied the boat, we got all our gear together, and off we went on the three-minute boat ride. Upon arrival at the site, we sort of looked in awe at the amount of work in store for us. The old lodge was tumble-down and in need of total demolition. That would start after the wood got there and we had our crews put together.

We grabbed our machetes, tucked our pants into our socks, disembarked, and trudged up the bank. Our main directive was to see the lay of the land and figure out how our plan would unfold harmoniously with the jungle. The actual lodge site was right on the inward bend of the river, making supply and passenger handling much easier. We had a big port, protected from the river's current. Great for fishing too.

The new lodge would take the old lodge's place, and we would follow the slight ridge on the bank of the river for our new construction, which turned out to be a very good decision. The land sloped down from the bank into the jungle, appearing to turn into swamp, which is not the best land to build on. From what we saw, it looked like we could wind our pathway around the big trees and not create much of a disturbance. We were starting out with our two houses, seven tourist bungalows, a large separated bathroom, a fuel dump, main lodge, kitchen, dishwashing area, a multi-story shop, and storage building. Over the next three weeks, until the girls came, we were only interested in a latrine, our two houses, and a walkway. The rest would be started after the girls left, and we would use the Dolphin Camp as our base until construction was complete.

We were getting kind of hungry. It was edging up to noon, so we headed back down to the camp. They had another great meal for us. A chicken *guiso*, a sort of stew, with potatoes and carrots, fried yucca, womboc salad, beans, rice and fresh fruit juice. About halfway through the meal, Lawrence had this great idea: take a canoe up the Cumaceba Creek. The creek emptied into the Río Yarapa, across from the Dolphin Camp. A great idea. We had all afternoon. The wood was supposed to be coming in that night, and we would start work the next morning.

We packed a little snack for the afternoon, unleashed one of the larger canoes, and pushed off across the river. A dugout canoe is a tricky little boat. You really have to keep your mind on what you are doing. Many gringos have been baptized in the Amazon Jungle water. If you are paddling against the current, and we were, you have to stay by the bank and paddle, paddle, paddle. If you don't you go backward due to the ten-knot current. We actually did lose ground a couple of times, trying to catch our breath, until I came up with a bright idea: paddle to the bank and grab the tree branches. The creek was a narrow waterway, very lush, and as we paddled deeper inward, the birds and animals became more apparent.

It was like sitting in the dentist's office, looking through an old *National Geographic* magazine issue on rainforests. All of a sudden you flow through the ink barrier and you are sitting in a canoe, experiencing with all your senses the wonders that only your eyes were capable of in the dentist's office. I'm talking about bird calls you can't believe, large snakes in the branches of trees 200 feet tall, a sloth slowly moving up a tree trunk, monkeys chattering in the upper branches, Kingfishers swooping across the water looking for skimmers, and some slippery river otters too.

We paddled up river for about an hour, and came to a small inlet that looked like it could have been overflow from a lake. We pulled the canoe in as far as we could and beached it in the mud. The small creek bed was dry, so we walked about two minutes and came to a small lake (later we learned it was Carmen Cocha, or Lake Carmen) encircled in prehistoric-looking palms. They were lacy-looking, but thick, with three-inch defensive spines all the way up the trunk to where the fronds started. I took a bunch from the ground. Very impressive-looking spines, thin, black, shiny and very hard. I had three holes in my earlobe from thirty-year-old piercings, so I took a few spines and fed them through. Quite the native son. Looked cool. I wore them every once in a while, but they were uncomfortable, and when I forgot about them, I stuck myself. I made a mental note that Carmen Cocha would be a great location for a floating cabin. Tourists would love it. Out in the middle of the Amazon Jungle, hearing fifteen-foot black caimans splashing around and jaguars snuffling on the banks. Everything you need for a restful night's sleep.

Pushing off in our canoe, I noticed a large mass of trees on the opposite side of the creek, about a hundred feet downriver. As we got closer, I realized that it was a jungle banyan with at least fifty aerial prop roots. Many were so large you couldn't tell which was the main trunk. I would say that some were between eighteen inches and thirty inches in diameter. There were also hundreds of small aerial prop roots, all grown together with laterals connecting them.

We banked the canoe and climbed up to the tree. What a great tree for a treehouse. I climbed up through the jungle Jim branches to at least thirty-five feet and looked around. That was the moment that my mind fixated on jungle elevation. I swore that someday I would see over the tops of the trees, and I did!

I also noticed that the sun was sinking in the sky, duh. Time to go. We probably had about an hour until sundown. We had about forty-five minutes of paddling to get back to camp. We were making our way downriver, paddles cutting the clear, brown water when I saw movement next to the side of the canoe. It was big…really big. Then it disappeared. Three seconds later it came by again, and I was able to get a good look at it—a huge Amazonian River tiger stingray (the only stingray in the world that dwells permanently in fresh water). It was flying in the water next to us, keeping pace with the canoe. This was 1992, and neither of us got our cameras ready in time…no iPhone. But guess what, I still have the picture in my mind.

We arrived at the Dolphin Camp just as it was turning from dusk to dark outside. The *mecheros*, open lanterns, were burning on the path, and the end of the day greeted us as we made our way to the Round House. There was no electricity, so the main building was lit with various oil lamps, a nice warm glow. I loved the look of the camps at night, with the spots of light winding through the jungle. I knew that very soon, that would all change. We'd purchased the best Aladdin mantle lamps in Iquitos, and we would bring extreme light to our communal buildings.

A quick, cold, river water shower, and I was ready to embrace the evening. Dinner, another superb feast, was *pollo saltado*. Strips of chicken, chopped onion, and tomato chunks, grilled, then topped with French fries, garnished with cilantro, and served on a bed of rice. Complementing this exquisite dish was steamed potato, beet, and carrot salad, and also a beer for me.

After this tasty treat, we worked on our art projects. Lawrence was making a staff with all the bones and teeth and macabre stuff he'd traded for the prior week. I was making a carved, palm fiber, toucan-head necklace with ground-found bird feathers and a *huangana* (wild boar) tusk for the beak. Later on, we stopped trading for all these animal byproducts. The people of Peru do eat these animals, though.

Carved toucan-head necklace

Lawrence had purchased some incredible battery-powered speakers in Rio to pair up with his waterproof Walkman (it played cassette tapes). We were rocking out to Def Leppard's "Hysteria," getting very creative, with no cares in the world.

– PART VII –
UNSUNG HEROES

The Cargo Boat Sinks,
New Friends

CHAPTER THIRTEEN

"There's been an accident!" Rolan exclaimed, running into the Round House. "The supply boat has sunk in the Río Yarapa!" Apparently, the boat had been passing by the small pueblo Puerto Miguel (our nearest neighbor) at around 9:30 p.m. when the pilot fell asleep, hit a submerged log, and put a hole the size of Rhode Island in the side of the boat. Luckily, he woke up and steered to the bank. It was 11:00 p.m. when Rolan notified us. No deaths, no injuries. We were OK. That ended our creative hour.

You know that the locals had to process all the information, decide what to do, argue a bit, then send someone up, paddling a canoe, to the Dolphin Camp to tell us the story. It all took a while. Now, we had to figure out what we were going to do. Our minds went wild trying to picture the scenario, what we needed, how we were going to salvage the cargo, and who would help us at this hour, 110 miles from any civilization. We just had to wing it. Our specialty.

Rolan came into our room as we were getting ready to go and reminded me that we had bought a few bottles of *aguardiente*, the local rum, produced at the distillery (on the bank of the Río Amazonas) we had visited on our way upriver.

Knowing what he knew (and we didn't), he said, "It would be good to bring it with us."

"OK, let's get drunk," I joked. "It couldn't get much worse."

Of course it could, but I was just trying to bring levity to our dismal situation. It was close to a full moon, so the lighting was actually good for what was in store. From what I could understand, Esteban had been in Puerto Miguel visiting family when the sinking happened, so he already had twenty-seven men working to get the lumber and supplies up to the surface.

As we came upon the scene, several men had flashlights, and it was true that the pilot had steered the sinking boat to the bank. The bow was angled up, into the muddy bank, with some of the metal roof exposed—the rest was underwater. This really was a long boat, and the river was fifteen to twenty feet deep, so the stern was sitting on the bottom of the river. Melanio idled the *Yacuruna* over to the hulk and turned off the motor. There were a few men standing on the metal roof and one of them was Esteban. He explained to us how his process was working. The men would pull one or two *tablas* (planks) to the bow of the boat, where canoes were waiting to be loaded. Each canoe could handle three to five tablas for the trip up the river in the dark. They would then unload at the new location and paddle back down for more. Soon, they would have to dive for the submerged tablas. The real kicker was that the trip up the river, and back down again, took an hour. Logistically speaking, there were 8,000 board feet of lumber on the boat—each tabla contained about ten board feet. There were approximately 800 tablas, and forty canoes to haul them. How many hours would it take them to move all the wood up river to the new lodge site? (This was beginning to sound like a story problem right out of math class.) I'll give you a hint: around eight hours. All night.

This is where we met *Filomon*.

We got out of the *Yacuruna* and were standing on the metal roof (of the beached hulk) when I noticed one of the divers was an older man. It was strange because most of the divers were young, but they had nothing on him, because he had close to nothing on…

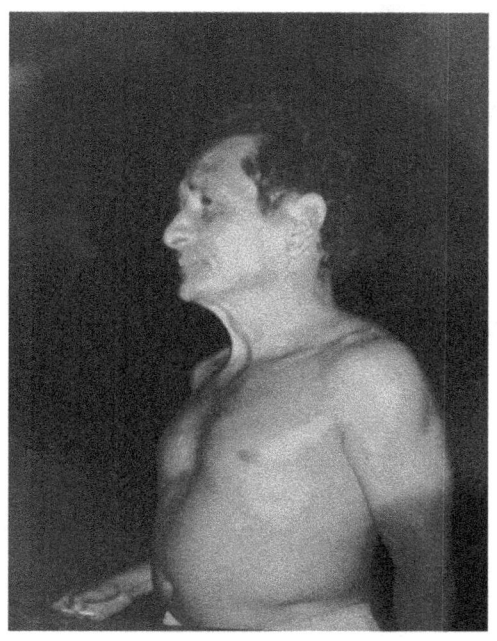

Speedo-type underwear, and nothing else. His face was like a road map, scarred and heavily creased, but he was strong and fit looking. The divers would take turns, some were pulling the tablas out of the sides of the boat even. They would rest for a minute or two on the roof, and then dive again. Most of them wore shorts and T-shirts, but not Filomon. They all looked cold while resting on the roof. Esteban told me, "This is the time for the aguardiente." He called out, "Hay trago."

I grabbed the bottles from our boat and passed them to Esteban. First one up was Filomon. This stuff is 180 proof, or something like that, and they just tipped the bottle and took a good long draw. Tasted like firewater to me.

If this was going to go on for the next eight hours, they were going to need more than two bottles. I asked Rolan to go ask the Bodega Bar if they had any. Of course they did, only at two times the price we paid on the Amazon. But hey, what ya gonna do? I gave him a bunch of soles, and Lawrence and I decided we couldn't be of any more help. I told Esteban to tell the men that we would pay everyone in the morning. We jumped in the boat and headed back to camp.

The half-submerged boat on the Yarapa

As we rode back up in the dark, moonlight filtering through the overhanging trees, my mind started working. Looking over at Lawrence, I knew his was too. It was almost midnight, but I wasn't tired, so we decided to stay up for a while and talk. First thing's first. We grabbed refreshments and settled down for a recount of what had happened to us in the last few hours.

Disaster, but only with physical things, advancing three steps, taking two steps back, still advancing though. Esteban promised me that all the wood would be at the new lodge site when we arrived there in the morning. The men would be there, finishing their job, and we could pay them. Serendipity money? If all this was to be proven true, then we really weren't behind. We would be on schedule.

We did have doubts though, being the bloated gloat Americanos that we were, and are, no matter how hard we fight it. We had these visions of our wood, a lot of wood, laying on the muddy banks of the river. All dirty and in disorganized piles... You know, "We know how to do things better than anyone else in the world."

Whether it be stacking wood, or designing buildings, we were, and are the best, right?

We went to sleep a bit stressed, thinking about the amount of work we would have to do in the morning, re-stacking the wood with stickers so it wouldn't mold. More money, more time, etc., etc.

In the morning we awoke a bit apprehensive. We ate breakfast, dressed for the day, and grudgingly started down the river to see the sunken boat. Pretty depressing, so we turned around and headed for the new camp.

Coming around the last curve (in the river) before the new camp, I saw what looked like a 1960s "Be In." People were all over the banks, milling around. Where's the band?

Then I noticed the stacks of wood. We were belittled by the pure ingenuity of our new neighbors. All 8,000 board feet were standing, like Xs, with plenty of air space to keep the mold from growing.

Stacked wood at the new site

They had attached logs between trees and stood the planks upright, juxtaposed back and forth, to form a long X tunnel.

Wow! We were blown away. We didn't have to do anything. The tablas were ready to use, and there were thirty-plus men, ready to get paid. These guys had been promised the sky many times and nothing ever materialized for them. Do this, and tomorrow I will pay you...yet tomorrow never came. (Wimpy and the hamburgers. "I'll gladly pay you Tuesday, for a hamburger today.") This mentality began in the days of the rubber boom in the early twentieth century. The *caucheros* (men who collected the sap, converted it into the crude rubber discs, and sent it off to make tires) basically enslaved the men of the various native tribes with promises of money and trade items. Some of these caucheros actually gave what they promised, while others just killed the workers and found a new tribe.

This was our introduction to our neighbors from Puerto Miguel. They worked all night in the cold, piranha-infested water, drank plenty of aguardiente (yee-haw), and were ready to drink more, I am sure, with the money they had just made. Did they deserve to do that? **Damned straight!**

I walked around their work, admiring how innovative it was. The sun wouldn't warp the boards, the rain couldn't soak them (the water just runs down to the ground), and I felt very small, like maybe two feet tall. These men were giants. The way we stack wood in the USA, with stickers (spacers), is wrong. The wood lies flat in the sun and the rain, saturated and warped, Home Depot style. Oh well, the only concession is, you have to stack it flat to move it, or ship it.

We paid all the men three times the normal wage for their time. I was still reeling with the understanding of what these men had actually accomplished. How could a person possibly feel anything other than respect for the outlay of energy, determination, and fulfillment these men had demonstrated? We were nonplussed. We would meet on the morrow at the new camp at 8:00 a.m. They all canoed away, and we stayed to make our next plan.

Meanwhile, Juan (from Iquitos) had been sleeping at the Dolphin Camp, trying to recuperate from the river trip. Lawrence and I returned and sat with him in the Round House. I watched as he prepared his coffee, stirring one, two, three, four, five, six teaspoons of sugar into the hot liquid, or should I say syrup? He looked a little worse for wear; it must have been a hard trip.

He told us that he'd had to stay awake almost the whole cruise. The crew had been trying to get into our cargo, and even the pilot was trying to use our gasoline. Juan told us that he caught one of the owners/brothers dragging one of our ten-gallon containers of gas away at Tamshiyacu. He said that he was afraid of getting thrown overboard, but he stood his ground, and what we sent, arrived. Thank you, Juan. I asked him to walk around with us and listen to everything. I had a plan in mind.

We would start the demolition of the old lodge, the marking of paths and the location of new construction. First though, was the induction of new employees...first thing in the morning.

***

Well, the morning came. It wasn't the best in the world, but a good breakfast always makes things look brighter. I called Esteban into the Round House and asked, "What do we have for today?"

"I have chosen thirty men from Puerto Miguel to talk to you and Mister Lawrence," he stated. "More or less the same ones who worked last night. There are many more who need *chamba* (work), but I will leave to you the decision of how many you will hire."

We had thirty warm bodies to put to work today if we wanted, and we wanted.

"So where are they?" I asked.

"They are at the old lodge site. They are waiting to talk with you."

"All thirty?"

"Yes, all thirty."

"Do they have tools?"

"They all have machetes."

"OK, let's go. Lawrence, what boat do you want to take?"

"*Yacuruna*, of course," he shouted, walking toward the bungalow.

The Dolphin Camp also had a couple of wooden boats with small motors that were made at the camp, and some dugout canoes (with machete-carved paddles) made in the village of Puerto Miguel. I marveled at them, as I had majored in Wood Sculpture in art school. They were truly pieces of art. I called to Melanio and made a signal like holding a steering wheel, then jerked my thumb upriver. Oh boy, he understood immediately and got moving, readying the *Yacuruna*. All boat captains sleep in their boats in the jungle.

It is a good thing that they sleep on a foam mattress, because you can hear the electric eels shocking the aluminum boats in the night. An ichthyologist (who came to our new lodge as a teaching professor) measured the voltage at 220 one night, believe it or not. You can see the electrical arcs in the water. The pilots always made sure they had their foam mattresses in the boat to sleep on. Grounded out.

Dimensional lumber is seldom used in the jungle. All building materials are round. If you need something flat (like a floor), a pona palm tree is cut down, which has a pithy center but a very hard and durable exterior. Sometimes it is divided into sections if the tree is exceptionally tall. It is then scored lengthwise with a machete all the way around each trunk section, and then beat with a heavy mallet until it cracks. It's then opened up and each flat section (approximately two feet wide by six or eight feet long) is laid on the round floor joists and lashed down with tamshi vine. These pona floors last a very long time in the jungle *tambos* (a dwelling with four upright posts, a pona floor, and a roof, consisting of a jungle wood frame and lashed down, dried palm leaf thatch). And no, it doesn't leak when raining—another great lesson. We would build in this style, what they call the *maloka*.

***

Lawrence, on the land

Lawrence and I had conferred at breakfast, just a bit, and decided that we would meet the guys and have some of them gather jungle materials while the others started clearing out the brush in the understory. Then we would be free to explore.

We were decked out—Banana Republic khakis (shirts and pants), rubber boots, Australian bush hats, and machetes. We were ready for anything, except what happened.

It was only about three minutes from the Dolphin Camp to the old, broken down lodge, which we were going to demo that week.

Norman in front of existing lodge

As we came around the last curve, there were the men, all on the bank, just like the day before. These men were our neighbors and friends. I think there were more than thirty guys sitting and milling about on the riverbank.

The old lodge was farther up the bank, and right there was a large bend in the river that formed a long peninsula.

I was raised in Indiana where there was a great deal of American Indian activity. As a matter of fact, my birth town was named after Princess Mishawaka, of the Potawatomi Tribe. There was a saying that I remember: *"Where the river bends, a community grows."* Mishawaka is a "bend" town.

Funny, my sister always told me that I had Blackfoot blood because of my feet. We lived out in the country and hardly ever wore shoes, except to go to church and school (and of course in the winter).

We idled down and pulled over to the bank. We had everybody's attention. (I found out later that the Dolphin Lady had told the villagers that we were going to employ the whole village. No wonder we had their attention.) There was one guy, still in his canoe, who had on a tourist-donated T-shirt that I recognized. A silk-screening company that I managed in Nevada had the license to print that shirt for Heavenly Valley Ski Resort, possibly seven years earlier. Small world!

We trudged up the steep bank and surveyed the scene in front of us. No one was milling around, talking, or even moving now that we had arrived. Esteban introduced us to the throng and explained the situation. Lawrence was going to give a brief mission statement. This was going to be very interesting. Lawrence uses a lot of twenty-dollar words, and I was hoping that I wouldn't see blank faces in the crowd.

He started with, "Buenas días, amigos," and then Esteban started translating, paragraph by paragraph.

"We have come to your country, and your village, to build a tourist lodge. Not a normal tourist lodge like you are familiar with, but one that will help you and your families, the people who live here, better your lives. We are projecting the building of schools, medical clinics, and micro-industries that will benefit your village, Puerto Miguel. We will help with school supplies for your children, so they can learn and grow into the twenty-first century."

I would just like to interject an insight here. The group of men Lawrence was addressing were pretty much all the same. No shoes, some with flip-flops, old shorts, worn-out T-shirts, and they'd arrived here in dugout canoes. Got it?

He continued, "You are going to help us build this lodge for a fair wage, and we are all going to learn new skills. What you learn will enrich your lives and give you a better chance to provide for your families. We only ask for one thing in return: help us protect the flora and fauna of this jungle from poachers. You can help us ensure that your children, and your children's children, are given the opportunity to live and thrive in this incredible forest."

There was absolute silence. I asked if there were any questions. Guess who raised his hand? Filomon. Remember the older guy in the Speedo from the night before? He started out with, "Cuando empezamos el trabajo y cuanto es lo que ganamos?"

That was what all of them were thinking. He asked, "When do we start work and how much do we earn?"

Lawrence and I looked at each other and both said, "Hoy, today."

As far as pay, let's just say we started all laborers at twice the amount they were accustomed to. Leaders were paid more, and the captain got the most, like everywhere. We didn't want to upset the delicate balance drastically, but we did want to start leveling out the playing field. We were trying to live by a new code, capitalistic chivalry — sharing, but not changing things any more than we had to. Everything we did was a dichotomy, of course. We were trying to create a touristic venture that actually benefitted the local villagers around us. Things would change. Nothing stays stagnant in the jungle, except the swamps.

There is a true story of a Yagua Indian village, close to Iquitos, that my lead guide, Octavio, the son of Chief Adolfo, recounted to me:

It all started in the 1950s, when a young entrepreneur came to the jungle

Esteban dressed in Yagua vestment

city of Iquitos, Peru with the intention of starting a "money making" business, offering sights and sounds of the Amazon Jungle. Of course, there was an ulterior motive in his mind, which I will not get into (almost everything good has a slimy underbelly). There was a village of Yagua Indians close by, and they helped him build the lodge for a pittance. They wore vestments of orange palm leaf fiber, known as *chambira*, dyed with *achiote*, a fruit in the jungle that is used as an orange colorant (for food also).

They had their chief and ayahuasquero, Adolfo Santana (a visionary who guided the warriors, fishermen, and hunters on vision quests with the famed potion ayahuasqua), tribal council, medicine man, and a tribal order which was adhered to.

My pencil drawing of Adolfo Santana, Chief of the Yaguas

When the small lodge had been completed and the tourists began to come, they were taken to the village to observe how the "savages" lived (remember, this was the 1950s). As time ground on, and no safety measures were taken to preserve their natural way of life, the Yaguas strayed from their heritage in lieu of the almighty tourist dollar. The Heir Apparent Chief, our guide, Octavio, left the village in 1967 to work in this lodge. I believe he was twelve years old.

I talked with Octavio, at length, about his life and how he arrived at the decision to leave the tribal order and pick up a new life. His reasoning was that he saw the future of his people affected by the grandeur of a separate reality, in jeopardy of losing the thread that had kept them woven together for centuries. He told me that the only future he saw for himself, at that time, was tourism. He

Octavio with a piranha

worked, taught himself English, and became one of the best guides in the Amazon. Octavio, as a boy, being the next chief of the tribe, had to endure rigorous grooming and training. He told me of the times he had to walk through the jungle during the new moon, dead of the night, barefoot and alone. He didn't make it the first few times, and had to be rescued, crying. Later, he noticed that some of the fungus mushrooms growing along the pathway glowed a bit in the dark. He followed the glow and came out at the edge of the village. He had passed one of his tests. He could shoot the eye of a flying bird with an eight-foot *pucuna* (blow gun), call birds and animals by whistling off of his thumbnail, and I've even personally seen him blow storm clouds away from our path while going back to Iquitos in the boats on the Amazon River.

One year we had a medical group at the lodge attending the six closest villages, and one of the more adventuresome members (even after my warnings of, ***"DO NOT WANDER OFF INTO THE JUNGLE BY YOURSELF"***) wandered off by himself. Nobody noticed his absence until about an hour before dark. OMG, everyone was freaked. We all knew what he had done. He had talked nonstop about trekking into the jungle. I asked Octavio to bring him back. He tracked the guy, not knowing where he'd started from, about a half mile into the swamps, and found him up to his waist in quick sand, boots and all. Yes, we do have a type of it in our swamp. Octavio cut some tamshi, made a rope, threw it to the guy, and pulled him out. They walked into the lodge. The guy was half mud, but he had a huge grin on his face. Octavio was his new BFF.

Unfortunately, the Yagua, Bora, and Ashuar villages around Iquitos have become spectacles. You can pay a fee and be taken by boat to the villages to see tribal dancing (in tribal costumes), dancing with boas, bare breasted women and girls, monkeys in captivity, you know, all things that should just make you sick. As soon as you give the tips and leave, they change out of the costumes, back into their T-shirts, shorts, and flip-flops, and go buy some aguardiente to make them forget. I have never been to a show in the villages. I refuse to go.

Getting back to the story, everyone on the bank of the river thought our deal was a pretty good deal. We had thirty or so men standing in front of us who wanted to get started—work, money, food, etc. I decided to give them a few ground rules. I started talking with Esteban translating.

I began with, "Buenas días. You will receive seven soles a day to work eight hours. Work starts at seven thirty in the morning. Since you are coming here in your canoes, try to be here before that time. You will have one half hour for your lunch, and will finish work at three thirty in the afternoon. You must be sober to work. If you are not, you will go home."

This really brought out the yuks, real leg-slapping belly laughs. This rule didn't work too well until I made a plank. Every man had to walk a ten-inch-wide board, eight feet long, riverbank to boat. If you made it, you worked. If you got wet, you went home.

I continued with the best part. "You will work Monday through Friday, five days, and get paid for six."

That was the winning ticket. Something for nothing.

"OK, let's get working!" I shouted.

We decided that we would go with the thirty guys for the first week, and after we had materials, we would add more. They were divided into two groups: one group in the jungle (getting jungle materials), and one group organizing the materials on the riverbank. Esteban was in charge, and Lawrence and I were free to roam around and get a feel for the place. This was really getting good. In Brazil, Lawrence had told me that I would be walking around with a riding crop.

CHAPTER FOURTEEN

We were trekking around, amazed at everything, getting the feeeeel for the place. Let me tell you what the first feeeeel was.

We were talking, looking up and all around. Lawrence was leaning on one tree with his right hand, and I was leaning on another tree with my left hand. We were laughing and making awful jokes (like we always do), when I saw him pull his hand off of that tree, shake it like crazy, and start yelling. I had just started to move my hand off the tree to go over to him (thinking he was starting some stupid joke), when someone hit me in the hand with a baseball bat (or rather that is what it felt like).

I looked around and saw that the tree was covered in inch-long black ants. I looked over at his tree and it was the same. Well, being good at math, I was able to put two and two together and got, "I'VE BEEN STUNG!"

We always carried poisonous bite suction kits in our utility pouches on our belts. I was fumbling in my pouch when I noticed my bites, or stings (whatever they were), were turning into white mounds. I looked at my bubba and he looked at me, and I could tell we were having the same thought. *DON'T LEAN AGAINST ANYTHING IN THE JUNGLE.*

I pulled that tool out of my pouch, placed that sucker over the first white mound, and pulled the plunger back. I repeated it three or four times and then went to the next one. Luckily, I only had two white mounds. I did the same thing to that one, then returned to the first, repeat, repeat, repeat. In my peripheral vision, I noticed that my buddy was doing the same thing, but when I looked, I noticed that he had more mounds than me. I looked at my tool and saw very little liquid in it, but there was some. He ended up only having three mounds, so we were almost even.

They still hurt, a lot, but the ungodly pain had passed. It pays to be prepared, remember the Boy Scouts. We both had a sting on the thumb, I had one on the back of my hand, and Lawrence had one on the back of his hand and one on his palm. I looked at my hand and realized that it was swelling rapidly. I hadn't learned yet that a urine/tobacco mixture neutralizes stings fast.

I looked at his hand and realized it was swelling even more rapidly than mine. We half-heartedly walked around a bit more. Having had problems with insects in the past, we weren't worried about dying. We'd just be very uncomfortable for a few days.

When we finally decided to join the pack again, our palms and the backs of our hands had exploded out to about double their usual size. We tried to keep our hands out of view, but the guys were on us before we knew it. Everyone agreed that it had to be the dreaded izula (bullet ant). This one is really a wingless wasp, up to one and a quarter inches long, with such a strong poison that four or five stings can give you a fever for a few days and actually kill an infant (they'd never heard of or seen the suction kit). I made a very heavily underlined note to myself to stay away from these guys. Of course it was impossible.

When I finally looked around, I saw that there were piles of thatching leaves, long wooden poles, and rolls of a vine. I asked Esteban what the rolls were for. He told me they were for lashing the *shungos* (posts and beams) together, and they were tamshi. One of the men, Poncho, noticed us looking at them, discussing the tamshi, and came over. He started conversing with Esteban. He asked us if we wanted to hear the story of the origin of the tamshi.

"Of course," I said.

Esteban began, "Poncho is telling me that when the izula ant is ready to die, it climbs to the top of the tree, dies, and its legs become the beginning shoots of the tamshi, which grows downward to the ground. They say that without the izula, there would not be tamshi for their construction."

In my mind, I could see that big-ass ant crawling decrepitly to the top of a 200-foot tree, falling on its back, and extending its legs out in the air. I never forgot the legend. Years later, when groups of kids were coming to the lodge every summer with every "ologist" professor you can think of, I relayed the legend to one of the entomologists.

He said, "That is very interesting. I have been studying the Amazon insects for years, and I know of the izula, their habitat, and their characteristics. I believe that there is a thread of credibility between the legend and reality. The seeds of the tamshi vine are part of the diet of the izula ant. When one of the village's more adventurous men climbed to the top of a strangler fig tree to cut the vine, he probably saw remains of the izulas and the sprouting seeds from their stomachs, and voilà, there you have it. The legend began."

I thanked Poncho for the enlightenment, and noticed that the swelling was spreading to my fingers. I looked over at Lawrence's hand and realized I had gotten off easy. His hand was starting to look like a blown-up surgical glove.

We had about fifty half-dollar-size by six-foot poles. These were for marking our clearing route. This is where the elevated walkways would be constructed. I picked four guys and told them to each bring six poles, translated of course. This is where it was going to get tricky — going off into the bush with no translator, as Esteban had to stay on the bank to receive the goods and run the show.

Jungle building materials

We grabbed our machetes, had our rubber boots, gloves (only one fit), and safari clothes on. We were ready. The only thing missing was the riding crop and the pith helmet. Carry on, carry on, boys. I was lucky that it was my left hand that was bad, and I could still wield a machete with my right. Poor Lawrence had to wield his with his left hand. Oh boy, I wanted to be nowhere near the sharp edge of that machete. We stood, looking at a wall of understory and brush. *Where do we start?*

For three days we worked, measuring, setting stakes, calculating, while the group of local men followed us, clearing the brush and raking the ground. By the time we left for Iquitos on Friday, we had paths cut from the new lodge area to the tool and fuel building, on to our two house areas, and to the first crude bathroom. We only had a few more weeks to complete our mini-civilization, and we were on a mission.

Jungle roofing materials

In the week that followed, we accomplished an incredible amount. Thirty guys can really do stuff if they are directed properly. Our hands became normal again, we marked and cleared three of the walkway paths, the first four buildings (remember, the girls were coming in three weeks), and the main lodge. We dismantled the old lodge, actually saving a lot of building materials, and collected an incredible amount of jungle materials that we would use to build the frames of everything, and of course, leaves for the roofs.

– PART VIII –
NEW YORK CITY TO STATEN ISLAND

Penthouse to Houseboat
1969

CHAPTER FIFTEEN

After Jay, the guitarist, freaked out and left the penthouse apartment, Larry and I were a bit shell shocked. I figured he would show up after the bad drug wore off and the lights came on, but no. He never showed up. Jeez Louise, we had a date set up to record a demo, parties to play, and streets to ravage. I had to accept the unacceptable. I was on my own. I called "the producer" to see if he still needed the bass player for the band, remember, no dice? Funny how some lessons come at a very high price.

I tried to back up John Sebastian's brother, Mark, for his gig at the Bitter End Coffee House, or some other Village Venue (I can't remember), but it just wasn't right. I couldn't keep my mind on his music. I was just so sure of us. We were going somewhere. I was derailed, lost and forlorn. I had to get myself together. I stayed in Thayer's 72nd Street apartment, trying to get something together, but my heart wasn't into it.

All this time, Larry was hanging out on a houseboat tied up on Staten Island. Thayer was there too, with the likes of people you only read about. I was in the city, reading the book *Beautiful Losers* by Leonard Cohen. A great book to read when you are suicidal. It could take an unstable person right over the edge. It was OK though. I was bewildered. So bewildered, that I went to a guitar store and traded my Höfner bass and amp for a handmade flamenco guitar with wooden peg tuners. It was a very nice instrument. I was going to force myself to write new songs, get better.

One day, Larry invited me to the houseboat for the weekend. This was not a standard houseboat, it was a 150-foot barge (moored on Staten Island next to the Moran Tug Corporation Dock, with the Kill Van Kull Waterway separating it from Bayonne, New Jersey) with a living structure built on top of the deck. There were six or more bedrooms, two bathrooms (not ecological, I'm sure), a kitchen, a 1,000+ square foot living room, big animal cages with big animals in them, and a very large deck on top. The people who revolved through this woman's houseboat (her name was Ronnie) were indescribable, but I will try in the next few paragraphs.

I have to admit, I either wanted something to happen in the city or I wanted to get out. Being on the barge for the weekend really helped me, and I felt less anxious and even relaxed.

One guy, Louie, came to the boat that weekend. Larry told me that Louie was a vegetarian, wore no leather, was the heir to S&H Green Stamps, and talked to animals. He wore a plain black suit and plastic wing tip shoes. He had red hair cut in a conservative fashion, parted on the side. I was pretty out of it, everyone was actually, so no one was really paying any attention to anyone else, until…

Louie took the gibbon out of its cage and started talking to him. It was funny, got to admit it. Louie would say things in his ear, and the gibbon would react, slapping his leg, waving his hands in the air, or acting like he was laughing (maybe he was). It was a good show. Later I learned that the gibbon was not a very nice gibbon. He bit, hit, and bullied people (Lawrence was one of his victims). I can't blame him, being in a cage and all, but with Louie, he was a real gem.

Another encounter with Louie was on his boat, *The Aphrodite*. He bought the presidential yacht, on which in 1945, FDR met with Churchill and Stalin to sign the treaty at the Yalta Conference (that was when they decided how to divide up the world). Louie invited four or five of us to go motoring out in the Hudson River toward Ellis Island.

This boat was really something. All teak, velvet, and gold-plated accessories. Sleek and sexy, powered by two very large aircraft motors, a tad decrepit, but river-worthy, for sure…or so we thought. Once we were out in the river, Louie throttled down and came to a stop. He opened a wooden trunk and removed what looked like costumes. Come to find out, they were old Shakespearian theatre costumes — velvet coats and pants, feather plumed hats, cracked leather shoes. He wanted us all to dress up and make a show for the Staten Island and Statue of Liberty Ferry passengers. Sounded like a good idea to us. He brought out an old, funky wooden case and extracted a bottle with a very ornate silver seal over the cork. Napoleon brandy from a sunken ship, supposedly. He had a case of it.

We powered up with the brandy and little purple pills, pulled the costumes on, and Louie headed toward the ferries. We were feeling our oats by that time, so we danced around on the ample deck, weaving in and out around the ferries. This was 1969, and most of these people on the ferries were tourists visiting from the Midwest. This was the stuff they saw on the news. Hippies, all fucked up, putting on a show. As you can imagine, the people on those boats were snapping photos, which fueled more dancing and mayhem from us. Everyone was waving and yelling things (good thing we couldn't hear them). When we had created enough commotion, Louie put the pedal to the metal and took off (like a jet) up the river.

Ronnie offered to put me up on the houseboat for a while to help me get out of the city. I figured I could have time to get it together a bit. I actually wrote a song on Ronnie's boat that I consider to be one of my best. A real jazzy number called "Moon Chambers." I'll sing you a couple of verses:

The moon has changed faces, in the shield of night.
Filtered down, between my fingers, as I tried to write.
The memories of thousands laughing,
Dancing to the rhythms in the street.

High above the city, Park Avenue.
My tunes were sung in phrases, from thoughts of you.
And voices burst through the music,
Giving verse to my elusive dream.

I don't want to lose you, baby, the love that we've found.
Just remember that love overcomes, the pains of the heart...
We know...

- PART IX -
WOODSTOCK

Three Days of Peace and Music
1969

CHAPTER SIXTEEN

One day, when we were all giant pillow lounging on the houseboat, Thayer announced that she had received free tickets for the musical festival of the century: "Woodstock, Three Days of Peace and Music." She had wrangled four tickets from a music producer, and Larry and I, along with her boyfriend Cosmo, were going with her. Note: this was before the festival. It hadn't transpired yet. It wasn't initially deemed the most incredible event ever to happen. We were just stoked to go listen to good music for free.

We all decided to go early, figuring to arrive in Bethel, NY in the afternoon on August 14, 1969, the day before the opening. A good friend had given each of us a two-inch-tall vial of our old friend, Orange Sunshine Acid. It really was orange. We arrived at the venue in the early afternoon, sun shining, construction of the stage going on. It was mostly just staff around the hayfield on the 600-acre dairy farm (owned by Max Yasgur). We just walked in, without being asked to show tickets or anything. They were not ready for the onslaught. I noticed that up on a hill where the entrance was going to be the workmen were installing a fence, stretching out in both directions. Good intentions, but it was only a six-foot-high fence. Back then, people believed in the good in people.

It was so peaceful and warm, we decided to ingest a bit of our "special" gift, walk around, and see what trouble we could get into. It didn't take long with my buddy by my side.

"Let's go see if we can help on the stage or get backstage somehow," he suggested. "If we can get in now, we may be able to stay inside for the whole thing."

We were already starting to get a bit toasted, but the two of us were known to ingest more than the average person on a regular basis, so we forged on. To this day, Larry holds that we changed numbers on our tickets to be "STAFF," and then "BACKSTAGE" later. I guess we could have (how would we have known what numbers to put on the tickets?). Anyway, after talking to a few people, moving through a couple of barriers, we were inside and ready to do whatever was necessary not to be kicked out. First we were on the stage, then there was talk of being able to ride in the helicopter, accompanying the musicians from the airport. By this time, it was starting to get dusky and some things were winding down. Not us, of course. We were flying high.

The building and sound system construction for the stage continued into the night. We were done and moved toward the staircase at the back of the stage. Maybe Jim Dent had been right, there were no barriers for us. When we reached the edge of the staircase, I looked into the menagerie that was backstage and couldn't believe my eyes (which probably looked like spinning pinwheels by this time). There was a huge, tent-like canopy. Under it were tables and tables of food. The best fruits, salads, cheeses, breads, and champagne, lots of it. We showed our paper and walked down the Golden Staircase.

Musicians had begun arriving, and there were tents set up for them to gather at and eventually sleep under. I snacked on a bit of food, drank some, and walked around, starstruck.

It was amazing how much we had experienced in a couple of

months. We arrived in mid-June, and we were now in mid-August. We were jerked out of our small-town reality, and basically forced to open and expand our minds for big city living. We'd seen and lived through scenes that we wouldn't have been able to even imagine existed. Let's see, indulge me for a minute or two of your time...

We hung out with dangerous gang members, ate hors d'oeuvres and drank sangria with people we'd only read about, played our music on the street and in parks where people offered us money, played music in a twenty-nine-room penthouse, which had its own art gallery and music room (along with two kitchens, two living rooms, three sitting/reading rooms, pantries, maid quarters, nine bedrooms and nine bathrooms). Not to mention all the other penthouses (one that was fully painted inside, artistically, by a Spanish mural artist on DMT) where we played our music at parties with maids and butlers rolling joints for everyone, famous musicians always sitting around, doing nothing but smoking, drinking, and laughing. We lived on Park Avenue in a penthouse and were staying on an incredibly domesticated houseboat where people like T. Leary, A. Hoffman, Super Joel, Allah Rakha (tabla player for Ravi S.) hung out. And at that moment, we were at Woodstock, the culmination of all our efforts. This all played out like a movie before our eyes.

Soon it was dark, and all the performers' tents were lit by electric bulbs. It actually looked like a Thai lantern festival, the ones with candle-lit white paper vessels that are floated in the air or on water. These tents were set up in the grass, and there were people inside actually playing music, and music I recognized, like "Amazing Grace." Yes, Arlo was there in one of the tents with Joan Baez singing, "We Shall Overcome." This was only the first night, and we were able to enter the tents, sit and listen, and partake in their offerings, mainly joints. Larry and I really blew a few minds with what we had in our pockets (a bit of Sunshine in the night). We finally crashed outside, exposed to the elements.

When we awoke around sunrise, the night people had been busy. I looked out to the grassy spectator hill. THERE WERE 100,000+ HIPPIES ON IT! They had come through the unfinished fence in the night. The promoters were freaked. The only money they had received was for pre-sale admissions. You can't charge admission without a gate. The show must go on!

At this time in our country, we were in a flux state. Drugs were a way to see past the mundane, into a better reality, or so we believed. Woodstock, "Three Days of Love and Music," was another reality. Five hundred thousand hippies: one death and one birth, a few overdoses, but nothing lethal, a lot of pregnancies (I am sure), Hog Farm cooking up "free food," and everyone (believe it or not) getting along. I ventured out into the throngs maybe four or five times. I saw no hostilities. I saw a lot of cooperation, love, and laughter. The Hog Farm was the best. Wavy was the first man I had ever met who was not a Hindu guru, but a real guru.

The first day was pretty good for us. We had to sort of stick around the stage to brown nose everyone, trying to move up in the echelon. We did! The first day we were sort of bozos, doing whatever was needed. The second day, we moved into press pit security. Larry and I were given Woodstock shirts and a heavy responsibility. We were literally the guys who let all the press into the front pit. I am telling you, it was beyond belief. The second day's music started around 1:15 p.m. or so. Larry and I had already gone out to the Hog Farm to get a bite and see the people. We walked around a bit and got ready for the deluge, you know, half a teaspoon of Sunshine... We be ready! It was a fourteen- to sixteen-hour shift.

The promoters of the festival talked to us about our responsibilities, trying to scare us so we'd stay aware. Pretty hard to scare people like us. *Life, Time, Rolling Stone, Newsweek, New Yorker, New York Times, Washington Post*, and every other big production mag or rag in the country was there. Even European productions were there. All photographers could snap photos, but no one could film except the future *Woodstock* filmmakers. They had carte blanche on the stage. Got it? Got it!

There was a gate at one end of the press pit. It opened outward. We checked each pass and only let in a safe number of photographers. Not all representatives could enter for every song. Sometimes we had to get the pigs out and let the lambs in. Who was to come in and when was basically up to an eighteen-year-old and a twenty-one-year-old. We got to know everyone very quickly.

There were real NYC off-duty police officers working the front of the stage. All were really nice guys. One especially cool guy told me one night, after he had dropped acid for the second time, that he could not see himself going back to being an officer in the city. I told him that no matter what happens, we all do what we must do. He understood that, but his job was difficult, I am sure. We had a high chain link fence to our backs where the people were. And the pit was about ten feet deep, so we had a buffer between the performers and the crowds. The Altamont Free Concert hadn't happened yet; almost four months to wait for disaster to happen.

These guys were all basically paparazzi, and they could be kind of surly. We had to be a bit forceful when it wasn't their turn, and all had to leave when finished taking their pics. When the bands finished, the pit was cleared. Empty. Next group, and we started all over again. When we saw a photographer just grooving to the music, he was out, and another could take his place. This was hard to maintain totally zonked on Sunshine, but the music was great, especially on the second and third days/nights. I mean, come on, ten feet away from the West Coast "new guy" was Carlos Santana, Leslie West, Alvin Lee, Janis, Pete Townsend, Jerry, Joe Cocker, CSN&Y, Grace Slick, and the very best performer (I listened to him as we were dragging ourselves out on the fourth day), JIMI! It was an experience that will stay with me, helping to mold my life every day, forever: "The Star Spangled Banner."

Just remembering some of the mind-clips brings back "ahh" times, like daily swims in the lake with 300 naked people, helicopters dropping water and sodas on the crowd in the hot sun with Canned Heat getting down. Bare breasted girls swaying to the music and "slippery slides" with mud-covered hippies having fun. Rain, rain, and more rain, with sun, sun, and more sun, people climbing the seventy-foot speaker towers, music blasting out at who knows how many decibels. Listening to Stephen Stills sing "Sweet Judy Blue Eyes" acoustically in a tent with the boys harmonizing...

I could go on and on, but all good things end and we had to return to reality, which wasn't much different, to tell you the truth, than what we had just experienced — just less people.

– PART X –
UNSUNG HEROES

Adopted Responsibilities,
Motor Madness

CHAPTER SEVENTEEN

On the second day after the sinking, the two brothers, the owners of the boat, decided to come to the camp and have a chat with us. I called Rolan over and they began.

"Señor, when are you going to fix our boat?" one said.

"The boat sunk delivering your wood," said the other.

I countered with, "We just paid you the other half of your fee for moving the wood. You have money to fix your boat."

"Oh no, señor, my son left this morning on the river bus with the money for our families," one said.

This was really starting to feel like a movie I had seen. They had drank aguardiente at the bodega for two days. This movie did not have a good ending.

"Our motor is under water and needs to be cleaned and fixed," said the other.

"Three quarters of your boat is under water. You have to raise it up, take the motor off to get fixed, patch the hole, and go home," I stated.

"Señor, we have no fuel and no boat to go home with."

I was thinking, *Shit, man, WTF.* I said, "Take the river bus home and bring people to fix your boat."

"We have no money," said Thing One.

"I'll give you money," I choked. Anything to get them out of our hair.

Thing One and Two said, in harmony, "But Señor, it is your fault and you must fix our boat."

I looked at Lawrence and he looked at me and we caved. Probably not a good idea to have enemies, not here in the deep, dark Amazon.

Now, the insult that went with the injury—they had to stay with us and eat our food for how long? Lordy be!

We had to make a plan: motor off of boat (ten feet below the surface), pull the boat onto the riverbank (just manpower), fix the hole, repair the motor, give them fuel, and send them on their way. Easy, right?

That put a serious kink in our plans (best laid, of mice and men?). Well, we were going to pull guys off to help, but the bulk of the force would be men in the village, ready to go first thing in the morning. Of course, we would have to pay them too. What I was figuring on was watching the progress on the boat, and when the work was over, adding the best workers to our crew. It turned out to be a very good idea.

We got the lodge group started. We divided the thirty-plus guys into three groups, picked a captain for each group (with Esteban's help), and started them on three different projects. Remember the construction supervisor (Cesar)? He came on the first (nightmare) trip with us from Iquitos. Lawrence and I laid out the buildings and left it up to him to do his magic. We left Esteban there to keep everything going.

We pulled away from the bank and I asked Lawrence, "Didn't Cesar look a little strange to you?"

"Uh, like how?" he asked.

"Like his eyes were bloodshot and his face looked like he was going to have a stroke or coronary. All bloated and flushed," I blurted.

"Well, let's keep an eye on him," he said and he patted my shoulder.

There is nothing like a speedboat on a river in the morning, with the fresh forest air (a hint of wood smoke) in one's face. Love it, baby!

We picked up Rolan as we passed the Dolphin Camp and headed to Puerto Miguel, ready for a real experience.

There were men on both sides of the river, ready and willing to work. Lawrence and I had a precise plan, and I wanted to stick to it the best we could. No free-for-alls. The first business of the day was getting the motor unhooked and on the bank. The boat had sunk on the opposite side of the river from the village. Someone had to actually dive down and disconnect the motor from the transom of the boat. Everyone was saying there was only one man for the job. He was a man who built his own machines, carved gears out of hard jungle woods, and ran the Dolphin Camp—the same camp we were occupying, at the moment, to build our camp. I had seen him at the camp and the DL had introduced us. Samuel, a very soft-spoken, pleasant man, with a smile on his face…always.

We sped back to the camp, and Rolan explained to Samuel what had to be done. He looked at me and smiled and said, "OK!"

Since it was midday we decided to eat lunch and tackle this bad puppy with a whole new attitude. Mmm, more fish, rice, and beans. You certainly cannot go wrong with that. It would have been so nice to relax a bit—we had worked so hard in the morning—but let's get 'er done! Work before pleasure.

We sped away as fast as possible, returning to the village to get started. Every time we saw a canoe ahead of us we slowed to zero. On these dugout canoes there was about an inch of space between the gunwale and the water. We slowed as a courtesy as well as for our own protection. Because of pilot negligence and a sunken canoe, I had to replace all the items in the canoe, the hardwood canoe that sunk to the bottom, punitive damages, and provide many apologies to the owner. All the guys were standing in the same places when we arrived. I wasn't too worried though, because I'd seen them in action a couple of nights before.

"Yo necesito dos llaves Americanos, y un desarmador plano y un cabo largo," said Samuel. He was telling us that he needed two adjustable wrenches, a standard screwdriver, and a long rope.

Melanio ran back to the boat to get the tools and the rope, while we were trying to figure out how he was going to do it. In the US, we would have either pumped out the hold of the boat with a temporary patch, inserted compressed air, or called a marine wrecker with a crane to lift it out. Alas, grasshopper, we were not in the US, and everything would be done manually. Lawrence and I were standing there, not really believing what we were seeing. We were the only ones in the dark. Everyone knew what Samuel was going to do.

He stripped off his shirt, bringing cat calls and hoots (quite muscular, he was), entered the boat in his blue jeans with the two wrenches and screwdriver secured in his pockets and the rope slung over his shoulder. He walked down the inclined floorboards and disappeared into the brown water... gone. The roof at the back of the

SAMUEL

boat was underwater, so we could only see bubbles surfacing every once in a while. We waited, and waited, and waited, everyone's eyes glued on the water, and then...no more bubbles! We waited again, and I was ready to jump in myself when he came ambling up the inclined floorboards, calm and collected.

Samuel sat on the bow of the boat and rested. Rolan asked him how it went and he replied, "No puedo ver nada, todo es por sentir," telling us that everything was navigated by feel because the water was too muddy and he couldn't see a thing.

To Rolan, I said, "Ask him how far he got." And he did.

Samuel basically said, to paraphrase, that there were six bolts holding the motor on the transom. He took only one off, because he had to figure it out. He would be able to take off three on his next trip. Up he stood, walked down the planks, and disappeared into the water again. Same process as the last time. When he'd returned and was sitting on the bow with three bolts in his hand, Rolan asked him (in Spanish), "How many more dives into the water?"

Samuel looked at us and sort of scrunched up one eye like Popeye and said, "Dos, tres, cuatro, no se."

He wasn't sure, two, three, or four. His next trip was to take off the last two bolts and start unhooking the throttle and the steering cable. When he had everything unhooked and loose, he could remove the motor from the transom, wrap the rope around it, and actually pick up the 300-pound, 100 HP motor and bring it to the bow of the boat. The rope was for the men on the bank, to pull him up the inclined floor boards. Remember those laws that we learned in school. That motor would only weigh 150–200 pounds underwater. No problem.

It took two more dives to get everything ready. He rested for a very short time, breathing normally, and gave the men on the bank the loose end of the rope. He looked at me, smiled, and began his march down the planks, hopefully for the last time.

He was under for longer than the other dives, and everyone was looking at each other nervously. All of a sudden there was a yank on the rope and the first man on the rope fell. Everyone grabbed it and pulled slowly, trying not to pull Samuel off his feet. Very quickly, not more than two to three seconds, we saw the motor break the surface, then Samuel's head. The motor was on his shoulder! He sputtered, spit, and took a huge breath while rolling the motor onto the floor planks.

There were eight men struggling with the rope, four more standing by, if needed. They pulled, and pulled, and pulled some more, gaining a foot each heave-ho. The other four men grabbed the end of the rope, and together they pulled that sucker up to the bow of the boat. Samuel was still helping, pushing and guiding, all the way up. They tied the rope off on a tree, and everybody laughed, hooted, and some of them even made the sign of the cross.

Samuel moseyed up to us and I hugged him, Lawrence hugged him, Rolan shook his hand, and everyone was hollering. He looked a little bit embarrassed. Of course we thanked him profusely, and that night he'd get his *propina*, or tip, for all the danger, courage, pain, and brains it took to pull it off. The eight men handled the removal of the motor from the bow and set it in a stand someone had made so it could be repaired later. Now was the real work, LOL — getting the sixty-five-foot boat out of the water and onto the bank.

We had to run back to the camp for more rope. This time, we brought one-inch-thick rope to pull the boat up and onto three strapped log balsas, floating docks, that someone agreed to rent to us. Much better than trying to pull it up and over the bank to the flat land.

The guys hooked it up and we used *Yacuruna's* pulling force to get the bow of the boat on the first balsa and let the water run out of the hole. We set up the second balsa, pulled the bow of the boat onto the second balsa, and let the water run out of the hole. Then we set up the third balsa, pulled the rest of the boat onto the three balsas, and we were there. When the water ran out of the hole, we were golden. The boat was emptied of water, the nasty, ripped hole was visible and exposed for repairs. All we had to do was repair everything.

It was getting on toward 3:00 p.m., and we still had to run up to the new lodge site to see how the crews had done for the day. We shut everything down at the boat site, hiring some men to start the repairs in the morning, and took off for the camp. We dropped Samuel, "our hero," at the Dolphin Camp, and continued on to our construction site. They had really made some advances. The main posts were set, the roof structures were being nailed into place, and they were working on the joisting of the floors. Lawrence and I looked at one another and smiled. We only had a few weeks left until the girls came from Brazil.

One crew was working on Lawrence's house, one on my house, and one on the latrine and fuel dump. Man, everything was looking incredible. Then I saw Cesar working with the group installing the posts for the fuel dump. They had dug the holes for the four main supports and were setting the *huacapu*, wooden posts. Cesar was looking at the guys plumbing the posts, and they were looking at him. I noticed that they had no levels, plumb bobs, or measuring tapes lying around. Lawrence and I were behind a small stand of trees, and I saw Cesar hold his hand up, giving hand signals to the post crew. *Move it to the left...stop...a little to the right...stop...back to the left a hair...perfect.* OK, he was doing everything by eye. Hmm!

I grabbed one of the new levels that we had bought in Iquitos, held up my hands for everyone to stop, and placed the level on the newly set post. It was a good five degrees off plumb. In other words, it wasn't straight, vertical. I checked the other ones, and all were five to seven degrees off. That would seriously fuck up a building.

I said, "Stop work for today, thank you!" Translated by Esteban.

Then I went to my house. Same problem, but they were starting to frame the roof. "Bye-bye for today!" I choked out.

Then we ran to Lawrence's house. Same problem with the posts, but they had the whole floor framed and were starting to nail down the floorboards. Very cautiously I placed the level on the floorboards. They were at least a foot higher in the back of the structure than the front. That is not level. Horizontal is in line with the horizon. I guess Cesar took it literally and followed the lay of the land. My foreman.

"Everybody go home. Have a nice night!" I said a little too loudly.

I snooped around and found a couple of empty bottles, sniffed them, and pronounced them aguardiente bottles. Boy, my work was cut out for me. Not only were there problems, this would throw us off another day. We'd get it, though. Tomorrow was a new day, and we were still young. I was forty-four, Lawrence was forty-one, and we still had a few weeks.

The sun did rise the next morning, I did get up, and we did get the work going. I'll tell you how.

After dinner that night, we created a strategy for getting everyone into gear and on the right path. When that was complete and we were satisfied, it was time for a little rock and roll! A little bit of Led Zeppelin, Def Leppard, and the Stones. That took us right up to dreamland. No snakes, and sleep was incredible in the dripping jungle.

***

Another beautiful day in the forest for us. Breakfast was *arroz chaufa* (fried rice), fried eggs, and fruit salad, consisting of tropical fruits, toast, jam, and local peanut butter. I couldn't help but wonder what our new employees in Puerto Miguel were having for breakfast. Jungle fruits or vegetables from their *chakras* (farms), or maybe eggs and rice, like us. Later, I would ask them.

Well, it was 6:30 in the morning and time to head on up the river to the construction site. The guys would be arriving soon and I wanted to be ready for them. Since Melanio had to go back into Iquitos to pick up the mechanic (from COREPSA) to fix the sodden motor from the sunken boat, we had to use a wooden boat with a small motor. We made our way to the site and we all disembarked, Lawrence and myself, Esteban, Cesar, and Juan. Early in the morning, Rolan had gone to Puerto Miguel to see how the men were doing on the repairs to the sunken boat. He had returned before we left with a list of materials needed from Iquitos. Melanio would pick them up while there.

I was thinking that if we employed Juan the next trip, we could leave Rolan in Iquitos to translate for us there, check on our tool shipment, and work on administrative problems since the DL was sharing her office with us. The tool and supply shipment from Miami was the most pressing problem we had. It supposedly had problems being packed up in Miami, and Federico had worked out a deal with Faucet Airlines to fly all of our stuff directly to Iquitos. That would be much better than a thirty-day cargo ship. We were elated that we could possibly have our stuff in a week. Dream on, little dreamer, this is Peru.

So, all the King's Men started to arrive in a canoe brigade. I held everyone up until I had the posse congregated, and then called them to attention. This time I had Juan translate, just to see how he would do.

I started out, "Friends and countrymen…" Just kidding.

"Good morning, friends. Yesterday we got off to a bad start. We need to begin every construction with a squared plot, plumbed posts, and a level floor." Everyone looked at one another uncomfortably.

Cesar was standing there and I had not talked to him yet. He didn't look too uncomfortable, he looked drunk.

"So," I began, "today we will start from the shungos. We will re-measure, level-out, and plumb-up everything. I will help Cesar today. That means, everything that cannot be rectified, we take down. The foundation is the most important part of the building. If it is wrong, the whole construction will be wrong. Grab your tools, go to your sites."

While I was waiting, talking to Juan, one of the captains came to me and asked, "Can we use a water level?"

He was referring to the Egyptian water level. The Egyptians utilized it in the building of the Great Pyramids, the principle being: water will find its own level. You use a clear flexible tube, and place one end on a desired level point, you have marked on the first post. Lay out the tube on the ground, and up the second post. Fill the tube with water, up to the level point marked on the first post. That will be the height of the floor. On the second post, the water level in the tube will be the true level point to mark for a truly level floor.

I asked, "Do you know how to use it?"

"Some of us do," he responded.

We were only able to buy twenty-four-inch levels in Iquitos, so this was a great idea due to the waves and ripples in the round jungle wood, and the thirteen plus feet between the posts. Another great lesson in the deep, dark jungle. Thanks, Richar!

We had clear, one-inch poly tubing for miscellaneous purposes, so we cut a long piece and off we went. We started at Lawrence's house since that was the worst one with the bad floor. Hugo and Richar, two captains, set up the water level. We demonstrated the real level, where the floor joists were supposed to be, and marked them on the shungos.

I said, "Unfasten these boards and situate them where they are supposed to be."

Next, I removed one of the plumb bobs from my pocket and demonstrated how far off the shungos were. I left them a plumb bob.

I said, "Straighten these up first, then do the floors."

It seemed to me that Juan was doing a great job translating. He could actually talk while I was talking, and everyone seemed to be understanding every word. Of course, we would see, wouldn't we? If this worked out, we could be covered on all sides.

We moved on to my house. They had to dismantle the roof framing; it was just too far off. I instructed them to start on the shungos, the base. Next, we moved to the fuel dump and latrine. Same thing, reset the shungos, get them plumb, mark the floor joists, and go on to the roof. The captains of each group took control of the square, plumb, and level aspect of the building, and I put Cesar on another job. I had the table saw set up because we needed the wood cleaned up a bit for the floors. I set him up doing a nice simple job. I figured he couldn't do too much damage.

Lawrence and I sat down on a couple of old barrels, drank water, and we were figuring out what we could do next when there was a loud crashing noise in the direction of Cesar. Anything could have happened, and it didn't sound good. We rushed over and Cesar was just standing there. The table saw fence was laying on the ground, twisted, the saw was off, and the blade was bent. Good thing it was getting on toward the end of the week, because Cesar was going back to Iquitos, never to return. What a fuck up!

I checked him out really well and he was not even scratched, just drunk. How in the world was he able to sneak that booze up there in the morning? Juan told me it was probably in his underwear. The boat driver took him back to the Dolphin Camp to sit it out. He could drink all he wanted. He'd go back to Iquitos on the river bus tomorrow in the early morning hours. Good riddance.

Meanwhile, I had to repair and make my table saw work again. I looked at it, in pieces. I'd have to make a new fence, check the motor shaft, it could be bent, and replace the blade. I was lucky that it was equipped with a circuit breaker. I removed the twisted blade, flipped the breaker, and plugged it in. When I hit the switch it hummed, didn't turn, and the breaker popped again. I removed the protector plate for the blade and there was a pretty good-sized piece of wood wedged against the motor shaft. How in the world? I had to pry it out with a small crowbar. It was really tweaked.

I changed the blade, flipped the breaker, plugged it in, hit the switch, and voila, sounded good. I only had to make a new fence. Mañana, mañana… There will always be another mañana!

CHAPTER EIGHTEEN

I checked my watch. Noon. I figured that Melanio should be getting back around 2:00 in the afternoon with the boat materials and the mechanic from COREPSA. I really wanted to get these boat guys out of my life. Enough was enough. Peruvians have a real good name for people like them: *conchuros*, meaning, "You offer your hand and they take your arm."

I had a good idea. It was time to check out the Dolphin Camp, eat lunch, have a beer, look around, and start all over again. I remembered the men coming to work in the morning, and not one of them had a lunch sack or box with food. I did notice a few women and children canoeing to the bank and handing off packages to some of the men around noon. So…I guess that meant that a lot of the men didn't eat? I'd ask about that, too.

I was starting to see that our two worlds were not the same. Running parallel, maybe, but two worlds with realities very diverse in nature. Our reality was one of basic stability with some variables mixed in. Their reality was one of constant variables, not ever knowing what was going to happen next. I have to state that we all do live with uncertainty, but most of us have options to choose from when the going gets tough. My new friends, like a majority of the world's population, had nothing to hold on to when their life went south. They are a tough, resilient breed of people with no constant thought of the future. They had to live in the here and now, because nothing was permanent for them in the jungle. They had very few "things" from their ancestors, since most all of their earthly possessions were made of earthly ingredients and decomposed. They disappeared. The older ones, like Mariano Manihuari Maytahuari, and Andrea Tamani Adirama, married since 1947, had a few tales to tell.

Born in 1913 and 1911, respectively, they lived in this area all of their lives. Mariano was the actual founder of Puerto Miguel. That is a story I will get to later, because they became a part of my reality. (Look for their stories in the sequel to *Dream of a Lifetime, Chasing the Dream.*)

Right now I have to repair a boat and build a lodge.

***

When Melanio returned with materials and technicians, we were ready to brave the New World of paradox. I was learning quite a bit every day. Even in the short time we had spent in the jungle, I already felt the process of protective scales forming on my body and mind. You have to be tough, wily, and aware to stay alive in the jungle, as you will see.

The mechanics enjoyed a nice long lunch and were as ready as we were to get started. We took Octavio, the wizard mechanic, and his assistant to the job site on the bank of the river and let them loose. They had quite a job ahead of them. The 'ol Johnson had been submerged for almost twenty-four hours, and we were paying for their services, so go to it, guys!

We unloaded the materials for the boat repairs and set the boat repair crew in motion. I watched for a while and realized that they all knew what they were doing. They needed no direction from us. We were looking at a good two days to complete the structural repairs on their boat, and maybe a day and a half to repair the motor. Octavio brought various replacement parts to install if needed. I was sure he would use as many as he could. Good for business. Sometimes you just had to eat it. I resist until the end, but when the deck is stacked and the odds are against me, I search for the fastest way out. This was it. I could see light at the end of the tunnel (of course it was only one of the many tunnels that we would encounter).

***

In the land package that Lawrence had purchased, there were actually two small lodges. The first, the one that we were rebuilding, we named *Campamento Dos*, or Camp Two. The second was up the river a piece, and we named it *Campamento Tres*, or Camp Three. We were including the Dolphin Camp, our headquarters, and referred to it as *Campamento Uno*, or Camp One. This distinction will make descriptions clearer in the future, when I refer to our movement between camps.

Lawrence and I discussed the subject, and decided it was time to really evaluate Campamento Tres. We'd stop by Campamento Dos to see how things were going, and then motor on up to Tres. We had our thinking caps on.

We approached the bank of Dos, and I noticed there were more and more materials piling up. Esteban was doing his job. The word was out and we were assembling an arsenal of Tinker-Toy-like sticks on the bank of the river. I could see now that we needed a full-time guardian at Dos to keep our materials safe. We had heard that things disappeared in the jungle. There was still one small building left standing after our demo job, and I decided that it could be the temporary guardhouse. It had great visibility and only needed the thatched roof repaired.

Lawrence and I walked around the construction sites with a few tools and deemed them all "level, plumb, and square" acceptable. I was starting to see what my life was adding up to be for the next X-amount of years. Was I biting off more than one man could chew? I knew that when the girls from Brazil left, Lawrence would be leaving too. Then I *would* be a stranger in a very strange land... Alone. I'd seen worse, though, so I trudged on.

With Campamento Dos in order, we decided to motor up river. We were going to have to decide what to do with this location, either recapture it from the jungle, or demo it and let the jungle recapture it from us. Rounding the last bend in the river before Campamento Tres, I noticed a small creek jutting off to the left side of the river, forming a nice V-shaped land mass. There was a stand of tiger bamboo and the lodge was nestled in next to it. I asked Juan to ask Melanio where the creek went. Melanio didn't know, and I imagined that it ran around the back of Dos, but had no idea where it emptied. Another thing to inquire about. Tres was in a worse state than Dos was. A sprawling common area, an outside cooking kitchen, and a latrine. The latrine had a white toilet that flushed with a bucket and emptied, from a tube, into the river. Not the best waste system. Dishes and clothes were washed on the bank of the river.

We decided that we were not going to do anything major to this location, other than send a crew to cut the weeds and clean it up. The family living there as caretakers were dug in, and we weren't about to throw them out just yet. They were protection from the marauders. Juan told me the marauders weren't really stealing. They figured if you weren't guarding it, you didn't want it, and it was up for dibs. Nice thing to know, a rule that I have learned to incorporate into my data bank. OK, send a crew up to cultivate and put it on the back burner. Enough going on. All in all, we were doing well. We still had two and a half weeks before our visitors joined us, and we looked at each other, sharing a sly smile. We were doing it, we really were, and with all the King's Men working, we could go back to Campamento Uno and catch up to this whirling dervish world we had created.

***

It was like waking up from a dream, or should I say a nightmare, relieved, but still consumed with the aftershock of events. Cesar was gone, the boat had been repaired, was afloat, and the motor was repaired and puttering away, headed down river. Out of our minds, out of our wallets, and out of our lives. It worked out just as I had thought—two days to fix the boat, motor, and kick their sad asses out of our camp. They were sorry to go. For them, it was just like being in prison in the USA: three squares a day, bed, bath, and recreation, not to mention the girls on the side. We were their BFFs, *muy amigos*, they were coming back to visit. We could use their services any time we had cargo, at a reduced rate. No, I don't think so. "Once bitten, be twice shy." They were disappearing over the horizon in more ways than one.

After Octavio finished making a new motor for them (with all the replacement parts he brought along) at our expense, we had to pay him and take the two techs back to Iquitos. Luckily, it was coming up on the weekend so they rode back to Iquitos with us. We didn't have to make a special (100 gallons of gasoline) trip. That felt good. We paid all the guys so they could drink old Julio's Bodega dry. We packed our gear, made our shopping lists, and took off for the big city.

Lawrence and Norman in the gallery

It was such a beautiful day on the Río Amazonas that Lawrence and I decided to sit in the open gallery in the bow. The wind rushing past, the warm sun on our skin, we talked and laughed all the way to Iquitos. I guess that we were having such a great time that we didn't even realize that we were in the Amazon sun. We pulled into Iquitos, got off of the boat, and were standing on the street waiting for a Motocar before I noticed that the skin on my face felt tight and hot. I noticed that Lawrence's face looked a bit red, and I asked, "Does my face look burnt to you?"

"Uh huh," he replied. "Sure does."

Hey, I'd been burnt before, pain-peel-done. I could stand it. We jumped in the Motocar and off we went to the hotel. When I was in my room and in front of a mirror, I lifted my hair up off of my forehead. Purple. My hairline, which never saw the sun, was burnt purple and it hurt to touch. I guess the three-and-a-half-hour ride going north into the sun with the wind in our faces wasn't the best choice. Sure was fun, though. I called my buddy and asked how his forehead felt.

"It's purple and I can't touch it," he said.

We commiserated for a while over coffee and cigarettes, ordered some food, and swore we would never sit in the front of the boat again. It was meant for bird watching and other tourist activities. We'd just have to bite the bullet and wait for it to pass, no Solarcaine in Peru.

***

I had met the three brothers on Kauai, when Larry and I were planning the beginning of our new project months before. They were three exceptional carpenters trying out for positions on the Peruvian Adventure. I sat in on the interviews to get an idea of how their minds were working.

First, there was Jak, a mountain of a man, young, long blond hair, and fit. His last job had been logging old Koa trees on the Big Island of Hawaii. It was clear that he was accustomed to using heavy equipment in the extraction process.

His brother Kevo, on the other hand, was a normal-sized human, long brown hair, older, and also fit. A carpenter by trade, he also had an outside interest: protecting whales. He allegedly had just spent a year or so on the front of a Greenpeace ship in the Pacific Ocean, attempting to foil the whaling industry. He had some good tales to tell.

The last brother, DD, was a master carpenter and adhered to the rigors of the trade. He appeared to be very intelligent, mathematical, but had a complicated situation going on and was not sure he could get his ducks in a row to attempt such a project. He begged off.

Jak and Kevo were interested but needed to think it over. I was leaving Kauai for Florida, so they left it with a, "We'll let you know." My feelings at the time were that they were a bit too manly for the project. We were not interested in wrestling the Amazon Rainforest to the ground. My thoughts were to look at the situation and devise a plan harmonious with the laws of the jungle.

Here we were though, picking up two of the brothers at the airport. They wanted to see the project for a hands-on decision. I really think they wanted a free trip to Peru and had no intentions of staying. They caused me a lot of trouble in the end. The plane was on time, we grabbed their bags, and Willy was there with the Ford, ready to go. Hotel, Ari's, and they couldn't wait to get on the street to check out the chicas.

We had two weeks to finesse the accommodations for the girls from Brazil, and these boys were going to help us.

- PART XI -
THE DROWNING AND THE FREEZING

Staten Island
September 1969

CHAPTER NINETEEN

It felt good getting back on the houseboat after Woodstock. Once you have sea legs and feel comfortable with the rolling water, the land has a different feel to it. Settled in, back with the animals, the people, and the ocean, we were in the groove. For the next few weeks, I messed around with my guitar, wrote some songs, and experienced a lot of out-of-body experiences. Lawrence, very social, was enjoying all the new personalities passing through the solace of Ronnie's houseboat, which was always open to her friends and acquaintances. It was a place to get away from the city.

One beautiful, sunny day, Lawrence woke up with an idea. There was an old dinghy stashed in the unused articles on the bow deck. I am not going to place blame onto my 'ol buddy; I admit that we both had our eyes on that dinghy for some time. We'd had harebrained ideas in the past, like taking off to NYC with a funky old car and no money.

"Let's patch this thing and take it out in the water," he urged. "We can get high, take some sandwiches, and paddle around."

"Great idea," I answered. "I'll look around for some caulk."

Reminiscing about it now, I know where they got the idea for the movie *Dumb and Dumber*—people just like us, except I do have to say, out loud, "Our better judgment was short-circuited by external influences."

We couldn't find any caulk, or nails, or sheet metal, so we walked across the street to the Ace and bought metal (probably aluminum) patching squares, caulk, and small nails. We did find a hammer on deck and took our first step into the *DANGER ZONE*. We flipped the boat over and took a close look at the damage.

"Aww, just a few small holes. Doesn't look bad," Lawrence said.

"That one is kinda big, but the metal is bigger so we should be OK. Let's put the metal and caulk on the inside and the outside of the boat, and then we'll surely be cruising," I added, self-assuredly.

We left her there to cure for a bit and went into the kitchen. Larry looked around and said, "Nobody's on the barge but us. I think everyone piled into the Saab this morning and went into the city."

"Better for us," I added.

We decided to bend our brains a bit, so we refreshed ourselves and made a couple of sandwiches for later, kicking back in the boat. Yessiree, the life of Riley. We were starting to see things differently, so we decided to get that bucket out in the waves. Everything looked good, so we flipped her over and she slid into the water. Larry tied her up and I found the two oars, not in the best of shape, but totally usable. The oarlocks were kinda rusty, but they're metal, right? Everything went in the boat — oars, sandwiches, some refreshments, water, and a couple of books. Were we stylin' or what? The best news was that there was no water entering the dinghy.

Now, this dinghy was not a big boat, not a Boston Whaler or anything like that. It was about eight feet long by four feet wide, more or less. One at a time we both climbed in and settled ourselves, which was a little more difficult than I had anticipated.

NOTE: I'd never trade any of these experiences that I am writing about for any others. I can say that I am glad they are over and done with. The lessons have been learned and we are better equipped to deal with the unexpected. AMEN.

Things turn kind of hazy at this point. One of us inserted the oars into the oarlocks, and I sort of remember that it was me, while the other untied the rope. We rowed out about twenty feet and stopped. What a beautiful day. The sky was blue and the water was polluted as hell, but looked OK from the boat. I was a little bothered by that heavy, oily slick on the surface, though.

A slight breeze came out of the east, and we decided to chill. We talked and closed our eyes, you know, sort of feeling the elements and not doing too much. I was rousted by the slight jostling of waves, opened my eyes, and quickly realized that we were much farther from shore than we had been in what seemed like a moment ago. Now we were both looking at the houseboat and not really believing our eyes. We were about sixty feet from shore and moving farther out by the second. I swung around and saw a black wall. I looked up, up, up, and realized that I was looking at an ocean liner.

In the middle of the Kill Van Kull waterway, about a thousand feet from us, heading east to NYC, was the 80,744-ton Queen Mary passenger ship. Apparently we were caught in its wake. Startled, I grabbed the oars and began pulling the left one as hard as I could, trying to move us away from the ship and toward shore. I was doing well, turning the boat, but then the oarlock split apart (remember, they were rusted), and the oar flew out of my hand, into the water.

We were in trouble. I had almost turned the boat away from the ship, so I decided to drag the right oar to turn us farther inward. This lasted about five seconds, and was working too, but the strain was too much. In a shattering of wood and metal, I somehow lost the other oar to the water. Now I had nothing. Even having one oar would raise our chances of survival tremendously. I did not want to be pulled into the actual wake of the ship. So, without thinking,

I dove in and went after one of the oars. I swam to it, only about fifteen feet, and heaved it toward the boat. Great, it almost reached, but Larry wasn't able to grab it. Mind you now, the boat was being pulled toward the ship, the oars were just floating, and I was trying to throw at least one to the boat. Well, it didn't work.

I swam to the other oar and tried the same trick. No dice. All of a sudden I realized that I was fighting for my life, maybe. I gave it one last try, swam balls to the wall toward the boat, and got nowhere. The current was too strong. I'd exhausted myself and couldn't get back. I was sliding in and out of the troughs, the ugly, black, sticky-thick water slid down my throat again, and I threw up. I looked one last time at Larry and our boat, and everything went black.

The next thing I remember was coming to, vomiting ugly-ass water, lying on the deck of a large yacht. I opened my eyes and heard, "He's coming around." Then, a couple of gasps and nervous laughs and I was sitting up.

I asked, "What happened?" A group of people were staring at me like I was walking to school and had forgotten to put my pants on. I remembered being in the water, and wondered how I had ended up on a boat.

"We pulled you out of the drink, mate," said one.

"We were scared to death you weren't breathing," said one of the women.

I just looked at them and asked, "Where is my friend and the boat?"

"We were watching the whole heartbreaking struggle," said an older guy with a captain's hat, "and started motoring over when you dove in the water. We were probably close to four hundred feet away, and it took a bit to reach you. Bobby, here, hooked your shirt with a gaffing hook, floated you to the stern, and pulled you in."

He kind of chuckled, and said, "You didn't look so good and you weren't breathing, so this lovely lady," pointing to a stern-looking, grey haired woman, "who happens to be a nurse, pumped you out. You feel OK?"

I just looked at them, wondering if he was really telling me the truth.

We were just pulling into the Moran Tugboat pier, our next-door neighbors, and I asked again, "And my friend?"

"Oh yeah," started the captain. "We chased after him, threw a rope, and towed him to that houseboat over there." He pointed to our home. "We were bringing you over here in case you needed an ambulance or a hearse," he laughed. "You're starting to look better. You want Moran to call anybody?"

I got up and steadied myself with the railing. "No," I said, "I'm going now. Thanks for saving me."

They all were smiling and clapping as I pulled myself up the ladder, onto the pier. I staggered, soaking wet and barefoot, down the wooden pier to the street, turned right, walked a few feet, turned toward the bushes, and threw up again — the most ugly saltwater I ever swallowed. That made me feel a little bit better, and I traveled the last fifty feet to the barge, walked in, and I felt pretty damned lucky to be alive.

Larry ran up and hugged me, and I noticed that my clothes were soaked, not in saltwater, but oily saltwater — black streaks and a heavy diesel smell. I showered, and showered, and showered. My hair felt terrible and greasy. When I was all cleaned up and dressed again (throwing the wet clothes in the trash), I sat down with a cup of tea and listened to the story of "How Norman Drowned."

According to my buddy, I had attempted, quite a few times, to throw the oars to the boat, and each time I was not quite close enough. I was treading water on the waves, into the troughs, over and over. Then my bobbing, oil-soaked head just disappeared, not to come up again. The yacht appeared out of nowhere and surprised him. One of the guys on the yacht was leaning over the side with what looked like a long stick, which turned out to be a gaffing hook. He stuck it in the water quite a few times. At first he thought the guy was trying to get me to grab the stick, but eventually he saw the man pull me up on a big hook, lifeless.

All this time, he was still being pulled into the slipstream of the Queen Mary. He watched as they pulled me around the boat to the stern and hauled me up onto the deck. Then the yacht took off, full bore, in his direction. They slowed, came up close, and threw a line, yelling, "Wrap it around the cleat on the bow."

He did, and they towed him to the houseboat. He unhooked, threw the rope back, and they left him wondering, *WTF*? Off they sped toward the Moran Tugboat pier, and you know the rest of the story.

I didn't have any death visions, you know, the tunnel with the light, etc. I was swimming, throwing, got tired, out of breath, and BLANK…until I opened my eyes and heard voices. I don't tell the whole story to many people, it makes me sound like a dummy, so keep it to yourselves. *And that's all I want to say about that.*

***

We hung out on the barge for a few weeks, went into the city a few times, saw some friends. Then one day, Thayer and her friend Cosmo advised us that they were taking off for New Mexico and California in a VW Bus. Taking Route 66 in the South to escape the cold. It was early October and already very nippy living on the water. I, too, had had enough of NYC and Staten Island. I told Larry that I thought I'd leave and make my way out to California again, pass through Goshen, Indiana, see family, and head on out to the west coast. He thought that was a great idea. Nothing else to do. We said our farewells to Thayer, promising that we would see her soon in San Francisco. I got a map and started plotting our route to Indiana. We still had a little bit of money, but I didn't want to spend it on transportation, so we decided to hitchhike.

We would be on the road again, for a few days at least. It all depended on our luck. Hitchhiking was not a certain thing, and sometimes a person could stand for hours and see one or two cars go by. Other times there could be a constant stream. That is why you had to plan your movements carefully. I decided to take Interstate 80 all the way to Indiana. Getting to 80 was the problem. There were a lot of intersecting highways, on and off ramps, and probably some walking involved to get to New Jersey, but there was always a lot of traffic, and we'd be sure to get into Pennsylvania by nightfall.

My main thought was that we could run into snow in the mountains of Pennsylvania. That would not be good. Ronnie always had extra clothing on the boat that transient people left behind. We actually found jackets, a couple of army blankets, and some more pants to choose from. Food, water, first aid, and warmth, all checked off. We were ready to go. Not the best time of year to hitchhike though.

We said our goodbyes and thanked Ronnie for all of her selfless hospitality. One of our boat friends used the little red Saab to drop us closer to Interstate 80. Good move. We only had to make three more exchanges to reach 80.

We were standing at the on ramp to Interstate 78 East for about twenty minutes, good weather, good spirits, when a 1957 black Buick Special pulled over, the chrome shining in the sun, windows down, and the radio blasting.

"Where you going?" the passenger asked.

"To I Ninety-Five North," I yelled.

"Hop in."

Two Italian guys, hair slicked back, shades, on their way to Newark for the day. I wondered if there was a body in the trunk. I figured that this would be just a half-hour ride, then off again.

"We're going North Ninety-Five too. How far up ya' going?" the driver asked.

"To Two-Eighty West."

"Hell, we're goin' that way too, into east Newark," he said, glancing back at us.

Hmm, what a coincidence! I was wondering if we were going to end up as bodies in the trunk. We looked at each other, eyebrows raised.

The radio was blasting, "Big girls don't cry, big girls don't cry!" Not our kind of music anymore, but at least they didn't want to talk.

Whoops, spoke too soon!

"Where you guys headed?" the passenger asked, turning down the radio.

"California, San Francisco," Larry replied.

"Aww, man. Frisco, eh? We just came from Philly. They got good tunes out there? I heard it is all hippies, nude babes, tits and ass and grass."

"Yeah," I returned, "I was there in sixty-eight, Haight-Ashbury, and I think you called it. Hippies and drugs, for sure."

Then the driver chimed in, "Oh boy, our lucky day...gotta guy here who knows the scene in Frisco. We were thinking of running some crank out there, selling it and becoming millionaires." They looked at each other and laughed, loudly! "Maybe we'll go with you guys. You want to make some money?"

They both glanced back at our deer-in-the-headlights look and burst out laughing.

"I'm just fuckin' with you, man. We got all we can handle here."

Whew! They had us going there, sort of on the edge of our seats, so we half-heartedly laughed along. Good thing I had my lead pipe in my bag, ha ha.

Up went the volume, and we didn't exist any longer. Thank God! Passing through the outskirts of Newark was depressing, and I couldn't wait to get into the wilds of Pennsylvania, beautiful and green. Before we knew it, we were entering east Newark and they pulled into a rest area to drop us off.

We scrambled out of the back seat and yelled our thanks to the two wise guys.

The driver looked out the rolled down window at me and winked. "Don't let your meat loaf," he said, then looked at his partner and floored the old Buick, throwing gravel and laughing all the way.

That was quite an introduction to our 650-mile journey back to the land of milk and honey.

We were a good hour and a half into our journey and about an hour from Interstate 80. We freshened up a bit in the public bathroom, did what a person does in a bathroom, and headed for the entrance to 280. A lot of cars zipping by. You know, it takes a special person to interrupt their journey and pick up hitchhikers. Boredom, loneliness, interest in humanity, good person, bad person, wanting to do well, wanting to do bad, or none of the above, just because they did. Imagine: two young men, dressed OK, looking like hippies, backpacks, a guitar case, laughing, their thumbs out, and it is 1969. Would you be interested in finding out what their story was? A lot of people were.

The next car to pull over, a red Cadillac convertible, was occupied by a woman, probably about thirty (older than us), dressed well, bouffant hairdo, and good looking. Things were looking up. She had her purse on the passenger seat, taken to mean, sit in the back. All people ask, "Where are you headed?"

"To Interstate Eighty west," was our answer.

"Hop in, boys."

We scrambled into the back. Black leather and red carpet, can't beat that. Everything was quiet as she pulled back onto the highway, but I noticed that she kept looking up, into the rearview mirror. I guess I would have too, if I was in her position.

"I'm only going as far as the Pennsylvania line," she said. "I live up there."

"That would be fine, ma'am," I said.

It was around eleven o'clock, and we had about an hour to ride with her. She wasn't talkative, but she just kept eyeing us in the mirror. She only asked two questions, all the way there.

"Do you play guitar?" she asked.

"Yes, I do," I responded.

"Were you playing in the city?"

"Yes," I said. That was it, no more questions, no more conversation, so I leaned my head back and recalled the memories of Haight-Ashbury.

CHAPTER TWENTY

It was 1968 and I had just finished working an art fair in Elkhart, Indiana at Partly Dave Coffee House where I had sold two sculptures. One, a small, twisted wire antique bicycle. The other, a foundry wax carving of Albert Schweitzer sitting on a stool, contemplating his fingernails. I hadn't sold the most spectacular one and was a bit disappointed. It was a full size plaster molding of me, sitting at a table, looking out. It had actually been featured in the newspaper article. Oh well, not to get sidetracked here.

I had dreamed of going to San Francisco the year before, 1967, for the Summer of Love in Golden Gate Park. I didn't make it, and lamented it the rest of the year. I figured that summer of '68 would probably be just about as good. What could change? I had a bit of money and two friends who wanted to go (one of whom had a VW Bug). Perfect, we made the plan. I was taking all my drawings to become a famous artist; the car owner, Lauren (he wrote the poem about my black, hairy cigarettes), was taking his poetry to speak at the City Lights Book Store; and Maryann was going along for the ride. Let's get the hell out of town.

We just picked up and left, leaving all our stuff at our parents' houses. It would be there when we got back. Things never changed in Goshen, Indiana.

All of us knew someone or had relatives somewhere along the way. We drove during the day, and sometimes at night. Sometimes we stayed with relatives. We kinda mooched a bit, I guess, but the relatives all seemed happy to see us. Go figure.

We came across the Golden Gate Bridge and could not believe our eyes. The city on the water, the sun sparkling on the ocean. We had arrived. Lauren had a friend living close to The Haight who invited us to hang there for a few days until we got our bearings. Heavenly. We found the address, parked the car, and bailed out, climbed about thirty steps, knocked, were greeted, and we were in. It was a big open loft with rooms in the back. Great friends, great view, great Scott!

The next day, I bought matte board and adhesive and started matting my drawings to take around and show. Lauren was reuniting with his friends, and Maryann was relaxing.

"Let's go to The Haight," someone said. "It's only a few blocks away, and it'll really open your eyes."

We needed our eyes opened, I thought, and cleaned up my mess. I was almost finished, and would be ready shortly to start my quest.

San Francisco was, and is, built on hills, almost small mountains. The streets are steep and winding. It was an actual climb up a hill (via sidewalk) to The Haight. It is called Haight-Ashbury because the center of activity is at the intersection of Haight Street and Ashbury Street. At first I was overwhelmed by the colorful clothes, the strong smell of incense, the head shops, poster shops, and hundreds of people on the street.

When I settled in and relaxed a bit, I started seeing other things. Things that surprised me. Everyone looked unkempt, dirty, stringy hair, dirty clothing. Was this the right place? There were a lot of young girls, I mean young, like under fifteen, walking around in a daze. No shoes, dirty feet, dirty clothes, with their hands out, panhandling (begging for money). We walked past an alley and I glanced into it. There was a young girl and an older guy, leaning against the brick wall. The girl had a piece of rubber tubing around her arm, the guy was sticking a hypodermic needle into her vein in broad daylight. In a single block, three guys tried to sell me drugs.

Just when I thought it couldn't get any worse, I saw a biker ride up, get off of his hog, walk up to one of the guys pushing drugs on the street, receive a wad of money from him, and pull a bag out of his shirt and stuff it in the kid's vest. I think I got the picture, especially when the biker got back on his bike and rode away. His colors read "Hell's Angels." It gave me the chills.

I was as far from a prude as you could get, but I had never journeyed to the dark side of life. For the first time, I saw the heartbreak and broken dreams of all these youngsters, and the greed and demonic business of the bikers. I'd read about stuff like this happening in New York, but that was different. There'd been junkies and pushers there for more than a century, I was sure. This was Sunny California, The Beach Boys, surfer music, smiling faces, movie stars, shit, shit, shit, damn it. I didn't want to be here anymore. This was the boulevard of broken dreams for me.

I learned something that day—about humanity, about me, and about the direction I wanted my life to go. I talked with Lauren and Maryann when we got back to the flat. We left Sunny California the next day.

Of course, I returned to the bay area, Northern California, many times, living there off and on for around twelve years (part of my Zombie Diaries).

CHAPTER TWENTY-ONE

Larry nudged me and said, "We're coming up on the Penn line."

I brought my wandering soul back to the present. Where was I? *We'll be hitching a ride on Interstate 80 in about fifteen minutes*, my brain told me. Out of nowhere, our hostess began talking again.

"Are you young men hungry? Would you like to come to my house for lunch?" she asked. We looked at each other, both thinking, *WHAT?*

I answered, "Do you live close to the highway?"

"I live about ten minutes away."

All the while, she was looking at us in the mirror and we were looking at each other, making gestures like *yes or no?* We decided on yes, and wondered if we had just become the luckiest men on the planet.

"Yes, I think that would be very nice of you. It is around lunchtime. I don't mean to be rude, but what is your name?" I asked. I figured we should at least get acquainted, you know, if...you know... if we were going to...

"My name isn't important, but you can call me Billie." She turned sideways, and I noticed in the reflective sunlight that she had a five o'clock shadow.

"You know, we really do appreciate the offer, but we want to reach Ohio by tonight, and it is quite a ways away, yet. I think it is better if you just drop us at your exit. Thanks a lot, though," I stammered.

"You sure? I have lots of good things at my house."

"We're sure, thanks again," I said. Good God, get me out of this car. "How far is it to your exit?" I added.

"Oh, just around the next curve. Too bad though, you are really missing out on a great time."

I didn't say another word until she or he slowed for the exit and pulled to the side of the highway. Then I opened the door and we hurried out, saying, "Thanks a lot, Billie. It's been real."

But before I could slam the door, he turned to us, and in a deep baritone voice, said, "See ya on the flip side."

I slammed the door and we watched as he sped down the exit, our mouths agape. Who woulda' thunk it? A good-looking woman in a red Cadillac…I guess it just wasn't in the stars.

We stood on the side of the highway in the midday sun, waiting for our next ride.

We didn't have to wait very long, maybe about forty minutes. An old Chevy pickup pulled over to the side of the road, and an old man inside the cab yelled, "Jump in the back if you want a ride."

I yelled back, "No thanks," and he jammed off.

Next, a blue '65 Ford pulled up and the window rolled down. "Where ya' headed?"

"All the way to Indiana," I said, looking in the window. There was a man in a nice suit, cigarette hanging out of his mouth, with a comb-over hairstyle, looking out at me.

"I'm only going about halfway through Pennsylvania," he said, "to Bellefonte, by the state college. But I'll take you as far as I'm going, if you want."

"It's better than a poke in the eye," I laughed. "We'll go." And we jumped in the back seat for about a four-hour ride.

It was late October, and most of the trees looked kind of bare, but there were still a few splashes of yellow, orange, and red amidst the green conifers. This state was really beautiful and wild. There were high hills that were almost mountains, and the highway was maintained very nicely. I actually recognized a few scenes from our first trip, five months earlier in the year. I was trying to piece together my plans for the days and weeks ahead, while Larry was snoring, scrunched up in the corner. The driver looked around and gave me a knowing grin. I thought, *His wife must snore.*

All good things come to an end, and our ride had. I saw the exit sign for the college up ahead and rousted the snoring man. I looked out and noticed that there weren't many cars on the highway. It was around five o'clock, and there was plenty of light to continue on. We thanked the gentleman and planted our feet on the cold pavement. We had climbed a bit in our journey, and the air was brisk and clean. Time to put on our jackets. The highway traffic was thinning for the night, and I felt the first tiny tinge of warning. We did not want to get caught out here in the cold at night. We only had two wool blankets and our jackets to keep us warm. If we did have to sleep outdoors, I could seek a sheltering thicket, back from the road, and make a fire. I was good at that.

About half an hour later, an old pickup veered over and we had to get in the berm to keep from getting hit. It skidded to a stop and the window rolled down.

"Get in," a scroungy-looking, bearded man said.

I looked at the sky and realized we had only about a half hour until dusk. Against my better judgment, I asked, "How far you going?"

He looked at us and responded, "A piece up the road."

We jumped in with all of our stuff on our laps, and when we were back on the road he looked at us.

"What you doin' out here?" he sneered.

"Just hitching through to Indiana," I replied, a little bit leery.

"You gonna camp for the night?"

"Oh, I don't think so, we're going to hitch on through."

He looked over at me, I was by the door, and he grunted, "Hmpf!"

What the hell was going on with this guy? He could be a problem, so I was alert, at least. After driving about thirty minutes at 60 MPH he pulled over.

"This is where you get out," he said.

"I thought you were going a ways?"

"Ha, ha, ha, I did go a ways, didn't ya' see?"

I just said, "OK," and we got out. He actually turned around, through the grass median, and peeled out, back the way he had come. The sun was just setting and there were no cars in sight. We looked at each other, shrugged our shoulders, and started walking west.

It was not the best time to be hitchhiking on an interstate highway. And I felt weird about our last ride. I had watched the movie *Easy Rider* before we left, and it was tugging at my mind. I kept telling myself to be aware of my surroundings. It was mainly tractor-trailer traffic on the road at this hour. They were passing at about 70 MPH, and I knew they were on a time schedule and were not about to stop.

We discussed it, and decided that the best thing to do was to hightail it inland, set up a camp, build a small fire, and brave the night. It was almost dark, and we knew we should set up camp before it became impossible. Off we ran, and found a small depression in the ground where a tree had fallen. The root system was up in the air, actually shielding us from the highway — just what I was looking for. There were a few clumps of snow around the forest, I imagined from the first storm of the year, but it reminded me that it could get cold at night. We could already see our breath, and my hands were getting a bit stiff.

I found enough deadfall to get a small campfire going and we huddled around it. We both had brought cheese, granola (hippy kibble), and water. We ate a little bit, tried to bring some levity to the situation, and wrapped up in the blankets.

We were actually doing pretty well in our little hovel, as the wind was blocked by the roots of the fallen tree. We were talking about the next day, and how far we could get, when I heard a vehicle skid to a stop about 300 to 400 feet to the east of us. Then another, and another. Raucous voices carried on the wind, and I heard, very clearly, "They're in here." I couldn't hear them running, but I knew they were coming. The only advantage we had was that we knew where they were, and they were looking for us. Luckily, we didn't have stuff strewn all over the place. I left the fire burning, we grabbed our shit, and headed west through the forest.

We were quite a distance away when they found our camp. From what I could hear, they thought they were going to surprise us. Well, they didn't. I heard yelling, cussing, threats, and a lot of pounding and beating sounds. Good thing it wasn't us on the receiving end.

We kept on running, and the bad thing was, we were sweating. Not a good thing to do in the cold. We kept running. The last thing in the world I was going to allow was a beating by a bunch of dipshits with clubs.

We ran for a long time. I heard an eighteen-wheeler passing by ahead of us, and figured that we were back near 80 again. Jesus, it had to be about 11:00, if not later, and the wind had picked up. I'd bet it was no more than twenty or thirty degrees out, and I wondered what we were going to do for the night.

When we came up on the interstate, I realized that no one was going to stop for us. The trucks were going seventy plus, it was dark, and by the time they saw us, they would be stopping 500 yards away. A no-brainer, we were up shit crick without a paddle. Sound the ALARM, find a place to be warm. We walked for a few miles, and then 80 crossed under another road. The overpass was high, and we climbed from the road up the concrete embankment to the crux.

The wind was somewhat blocked by the overpass, and all we had to deal with was the ambient cold. At the very top there was a leveling off, and we could both fit on the platform but we had to be very close together. It was not the best scenario we could have imagined, but *did we want to survive the night?* It was below freezing. We still had six hours until dawn, like it or lump it. We laid one blanket under us because the concrete was like ice, snuggled as close as we could, wrapped the other blanket over us, and prayed morning would come.

Believe it or not, we woke up in the morning light. (Of course we did, or I wouldn't be writing this.) Everything was stiff. I could barely move my arm from around Larry's body. We disengaged, looking at each other, grabbed our stuff, and slid down the concrete embankment. When we reached the bottom, we just sat there for a moment in shock. We were still breathing. Don't get me wrong, we were frozen. Teeth chattering. Bones creaking. We just draped the blankets over our shoulders, grabbed our packs and my poor guitar, and stood by the edge of the secondary road.

We watched an eighteen-wheeler come into view about a half mile away. It didn't matter which way he was going, we just needed to get warm. We started waving our arms, trying to attract his attention. I heard the distinctive sound of deceleration, and then braking. I could not believe it. We were saved.

There was nothing more beautiful than this seventy-foot monster stopping next to us. The driver placed it in neutral, slid over to the passenger window, rolled it down, and said, "You boys look cold."

We laughed as best we could, and he said, "Hop in." As he opened the door, the heat rushed out to us and we climbed up.

"There's a truck stop about two miles up this road. I'm sure I can talk them into a shower for you two," he said, smiling.

He asked, and I told him the whole sordid tale before we reached the stop. All he could say was, "That was quite a night for you boys."

His truck was very warm, and we were pretty well thawed out, so he asked what we wanted to do first, eat or shower.

We had our hot showers and he even treated us to breakfast. I told him that we had money, and he said, "It's not every day I get this type of excitement. I'm willing to pay for it, thanks. It was my pleasure." What a savior.

Unfortunately, he was going east, and we were going west, so we parted company, walked out to Highway 80, and we started our day with the morning sun. We stuck out our thumbs, almost 350 miles from our destination. We had broken the hex of bad rides. We overcame something that we were not even aware of. All of the three remaining rides were uneventful, inconsequential, and eeeeeeasy.

Eight hours later, we were calling a friend to pick us up at the toll house outside of Goshen. Yeeeeeeeeeeeee-haw! We were back.

- PART XII -
READY OR NOT!

The Girls of Brazil Are Coming

CHAPTER TWENTY-TWO

Three and a half weeks of hard work, and we had completed our projections. It was Thursday morning, and we had a day and a half to fine tune anything that was out of line. We had completed my house, Lawrence's house, the latrine, a fuel shack, and a walkway to our two houses. We were feeling pretty good. We were happy with the work our guys had done, and the brothers had worked well with their expertise, building the beds, doors, shelves, and a screened cabinet for some food, giving us the time we needed to prepare and work on future plans.

The only problem was, when we went to Iquitos for the weekends, the boys were a little rowdy. Jak was cool, liked to rent motorcycles, and already had a steady girlfriend who was maybe sixteen or seventeen years old. They'd race around the city on the rented motorcycle and dance at night. Drink a lot of beer, too. Jak was having a good time.

Kevo was a little different. He was deep and had

My house on the Río Yarapa

Inside my house

a lot of underlying currents to deal with. I really never knew what he was thinking, and he had a bit of an ego problem. Pretty opaque.

By Friday, we were ready to take off for Iquitos and a little R&R. We stayed out of the front gallery of the *Yacuruna* on the trip down the Río Amazonas. There were four nice upholstered seats in the boat, and I had made a nice bench seat for the stern. Melanio, Juan, Jak, Kevo, Lawrence and I fit in quite comfortably. On the way back out to the Yarapa, I guess the girls would have to sit on our laps. Ho, ho, ho.

The walkway to our houses

Everyone scattered when we reached Iquitos. It was Friday afternoon, and each of us had different desires after a week in the jungle. The girls were arriving on Varig Airlines the next day, Saturday, in the afternoon. One of our old high school friends was due to arrive from Miami in the morning. It was going to be a great day—a lot of running around, but we were ready for it. We finished the day by eating at Ari's, planning our tomorrow, and walking around the plaza.

***

The ride to the airport with Willy and his beat-up Ford was reckless and hectic. Our friend Joey arrived. Customs and immigration were no problem, and it was a gas. I had seen him three years earlier at his high school reunion, but we really hadn't had enough time. This was going to be a good two weeks, although I knew what I had to look forward to: friends, fun, games, diversion, all the trimmings, and then, everyone was going to leave. I would be on my own. Good thing I enjoyed talking to myself.

We got Joey settled in his hotel room, had lunch at Ari's to knock his socks off, and the three of us talked *old times...high school daze!* Joey had become quite the photographer. He was putting together a black-and-white "Photographic Journal" of our new project. Cool! We laughed and jawed right up to the time we jumped in Willy's Ford to go pick up the girls.

In those days, Varig Airlines brought quite a few passengers to Iquitos. Most were from Manaus, the Santeria jungle town in the Brazilian Amazon, rather than from Rio on the Atlantic coast. At the time I didn't realize why, but later it became apparent when there was a huge gold scandal and exposé.

Brazilians were paying *coima* (bribes) to obtain false documents to mine for gold in the Peruvian Amazon. Water is needed to process the ore, and the refuse and tailings end up in the river, poisoning the villagers' water supplies with mercury, arsenic, and lead.

The girls weren't mining for gold, but they were definitely mining. We could see them from the minute they stepped out onto the stairs. Skin-tight blue jeans and Lycra tank tops, great figures, and laughing, they stood out like stars in a night sky. I could see that Lawrence was smitten, and so happy to have his girl, Adriana, there. On the other hand, I was happy, but still fighting with my angels and demons. I realized, at that point, if I were to have any type of a relationship with a woman here in the jungle, it would have to be someone local. I was not going to have another long-distance relationship. I had lived three times with the loneliness, stress, and strain it creates in one's life.

Same drill from Brazil, customs, immigration, National Police, and there they were. We all greeted and exchanged *mhuas* all around (what a great custom). Lawrence and his girl looked like Siamese twins. I guess that lapsed time was really difficult for them. I was wondering what my girl Vanda and I looked like. Friends, maybe more? We were happy to see the girls arrive after all the hoopla.

Between the two of them, there were five large suitcases for two weeks in the jungle. I couldn't wait to see all the surprises up their dresses—sorry, I meant up their sleeves, you know…magic tricks…oh well, forget it! We shoved them in the trunk (the suitcases, not the girls), and Willy honked and weaved his way back to the hotel.

We all agreed to take an hour to rest, shower, and then meet back in the lobby to have some early dinner. We figured that would be enough time to re-acquaint and get spruced up. The Hotel Acosta was nothing like the Benidorm in Rio. No saunas, Jacuzzis, a limited frio bar, and bad beds, but we made it work and we all met up in the lobby an hour later.

We had gained a bit of notoriety after being in Iquitos for a month, and I'm sure everyone thought we were gay since we did not have women on our arms all of the time. Now we did…and they were knockouts. There were a lot of foreign ex-pats in Iquitos because it was kind of like the frontier—not a lot of restrictions on your behavior — and when we strolled into Ari's, believe me, ALL EYES WERE ON US.

Juan was there picking up a few extra bucks from the new marks arriving on the planes. The minute he saw us he ran over, wanting to be introduced to the girls. We had been talking about them since we met him, and now they were a reality. He also wanted to make sure that he was going back out to the camp with us on Sunday. We assured him that he was, and asked for a bit of privacy. He still finagled a way to be our waiter, the crafty guy.

We dined on our favorites as the girls side-glanced the crudeness of the restaurant, but they could not dispute the taste of the *paiche a la loretana*.

Ari prepared the very best, and the portions were very generous. Everyone was cool, and after a while, the locals became accustomed to the new faces and stopped staring. Joey, on the other hand, was in the market for a girl, and all the waitresses were very friendly with him. They were also working and couldn't be wooed too much until after midnight. He'd be asleep by then. Maybe he would find a sweetheart out in the jungle.

CHAPTER TWENTY-THREE

We left port at midday, had lunch to-go from Ari's and an overloaded boat. It would take us a bit longer than our usual three and a half hours because of the extra weight. No problem, we were on schedule and would be there by 4:00 or 4:30. Just sit back, relax, and enjoy the soft flesh leaning into me. Yeah, baby!

No distress today. We tied the boat up at 4:25 in the afternoon, walked up to Camp One, introduced everyone to everyone, and decided to go upriver to our new houses before dinner.

Our crew had worked hard, and the place looked good. Our new guardian/security officer (Juan's brother-in-law, Frank, ha-ha) was stationed at the fuel dump. As we walked down the new walkway to our rooms, I wondered when the stark reality would set in. *Latrine…gotta go to the bathroom, uh-oh!*

We weren't worrying *too* much; these girls had grown up in the small villages and moved to Rio later. It was definitely a far cry from the Benidorm Hotel. Were they troopers? We'd see. We did have chamber pots for the night and the easy stuff. We *were* thoughtful.

An hour later, sweaty and in need of a shower, we made our way back to Camp One. Ahh, cold showers, a good meal, and back up to our houses for another round and a good night's sleep in the deep, dark jungle, with all the sounds and the animals prowling around. The one thing that made it all worthwhile was rounding that last turn in the river and seeing Camp Two all lit up with torches. This wasn't fake, it was the real outdoor experience. We were creating it *and* living it.

***

Breakfast was at a certain time at Camp One, and the workers would be trickling in at about seven to Camp Two. We had made tentative plans the night before to get up and head to Camp One as soon as we heard the canoes on the river in front of our houses. Well, I was hearing them, but no one else was up. Vanda was not moving. I called out (not too loudly), "Lawrence," and got no answer. OK, I decided to get up and see how everything was stacking up for the day.

Well, the first thing that set me off was that there was no coffee. I'd have to remedy that. The first thing in my day was always a cup of Joe. I grumbled down the walkway, greeted Frank, walked down the bank, and watched the workers paddling upriver. I heard a boat with a small motor trudging toward us, and figured it was Esteban, coming to work at Camp Two. I waited, identified Esteban, turned, and walked back up the bank. I heard him calling to me, "Señor Norman, Señor Norman."

I turned around and saw that he was carrying a pump Thermos in a box. I guess I shouldn't have jumped to conclusions; everyone knew what I did in the morning. He had cups, spoons, milk, and sugar, and the coffee was hot. I could have hugged him (American gratitude), but they weren't quite ready for that yet.

None of the workers, or Jak and Kevo, or even Joey, had ever seen such a display of seductive femininity, so the girls were quite a spectacle. Even walking from the houses to the boat drew everyone's attention. The five suitcases contained very provocative clothing, a lot of Lycra, very tight shorts and pants, and stylish shoes. There wasn't a lot of concern with makeup. Natural beauty seemed to rule. Who needed flashy makeup when you had those bodies?

I met with Esteban and set the day in motion with clearing and cleanup. We were going to start the construction of the main lodge, and we needed to order more jungle materials. The girls and Joey were going to be with us in the jungle for one and a half weeks. We wanted to enjoy ourselves, and I didn't want to be working every day. I planned to meet with Esteban each morning, and if there were problems or building questions, I would clarify and demonstrate before anyone awoke. The brothers were going to help keep everything running smoothly. I already noticed that I would have to watch Kevo. He seemed to be a bit rigid, and really wanted to be a boss of many. He was also overly interested in Vanda. Oh well, c'est la vie.

I have to mention here, that some of these guys were incredible builders in the jungle style. I never thought that I was teaching them to build. They were teaching me how to build, and I was refining the style a bit to create our building design. This was always meant to be a symbiotic relationship, and all of us definitely benefited handsomely. In our main construction boom, which spanned one year and nine months, we employed ninety-six people from the village of Puerto Miguel. Mostly men (of course), but women also.

Meandering my way back to the story, we planned to go to a village to visit a tribe of people who had relocated from Ecuador years before. They were called Jivaro, and also Ashuar, and in times past, they were famous for their headhunting and shrinking of heads. The Jivaro are the only tribe known to have revolted and defeated the Spanish Conquistadores, and were never conquered by the Spaniards, and their gold (?) was never confiscated for they had none. The Spaniards never found the famous El Dorado, city of gold, in the Amazon that they lusted after.

Ramon, the leader and shaman of the village, was a very amicable man who welcomed everyone to his village, which was called Nuevo Jerusalem, or New Jerusalem. I never asked what the significance of the name was; I didn't want them to shrink my head. Just kidding. We were to be boating down river for about a half an hour, and trekking through the jungle for another half an hour to introduce ourselves to the village. We had heard that the village was one of the poorest in the area, and there were only about thirteen families. All were in the same destitute situation. Let's go cheer them up, we thought.

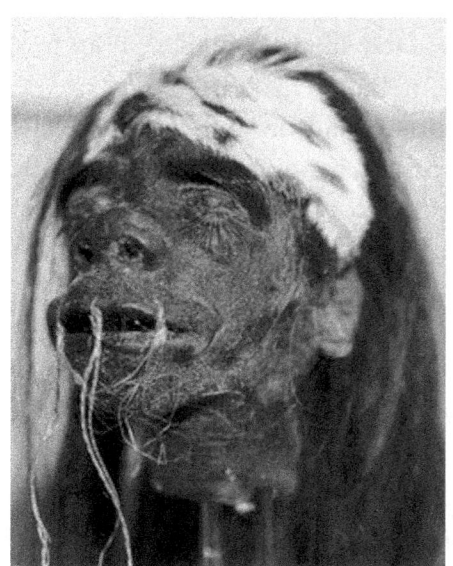
Jivaro shrunken head

Everyone was working well at Camp Two, so we decided to take Esteban with us as guide and translator. It was a good move. We disembarked at another village named Jaldar, and Vanda was not happy about wearing the knee-high rubber boots and decided to wear her white leather tennis shoes. I warned her that they would get nasty, but she insisted. We embarked on the trail, no more than a one-foot-wide slash in the underbrush, and halfway to the village I looked at the white shoes and they were still white. On the other hand, our boots were muddy, but it could have been due to the fact that I helped her across every stream and mud hole we came to.

We did reach the village, and when we entered the village perimeter, the first thing we saw was a stretched baby jaguar skin, and someone was broiling a small caiman (Alligatoridae) over a wood fire. We were not in Kansas, or Rio, for that matter. Esteban called out in a respectful tone, and Ramon appeared at his porch. This was the Ramon I will remember.

All the houses were constructed in the Maloka style, four posts, floor, and thatched roof. In Ramon's house, four or five women were sitting in a circle, dried mud on their feet and legs, wearing very worn and soiled dresses, chewing on pieces of a soft, white, fibrous stick that looked like it had been cooked. They each chewed for a considerable amount of time, and then spit the liquid into a hollowed out, oblong-shaped wooden bowl. Over and over and over they chewed and spit. The bowl probably held three gallons or more, and it was at least half full. I had my own ideas as to what they were doing, but I figured it was better to ask Esteban to explain since five strangers were staring at them with their mouths open, duh.

Shaman Ramon
Photo by Patty Webster

"What are they making, Esteban?" I asked.

"They are preparing the *masato*. A fermented drink from yuca that is slightly alcoholic. Everyone drinks it throughout the day," he explained.

"They're chewing it, though," offered Joey.

I looked at our girls and said, "No Coca-Cola here," pointed at the floor, and everyone chuckled, except our girls.

Esteban began, "The masato is their main beverage, and it is believed to kill bad bacteria because of the fermentation process. The women chew it so it mixes with their saliva, and that starts the process. It usually sits for a day or so, depending on how strong they drink it. It is said that Ramon's wife makes the sweetest masato."

I looked over at the very old woman with tousled grey hair, slightly overweight, many lines in her beautiful face, and when she smiled at me (not understanding a single word), she had two teeth, one up and one down. Her smile was angelic, and she twisted my heart. This was one of many heartbreaks I would endure, coming from the land of plenty.

Special Note

From my point of view, people less fortunate than myself were not *untouchables*. Just the opposite. My experiences in this world taught me that beneficence was the true path to travel. Growing up in the very rural part of northern Indiana, there was a stretch in my youth (after my parents' divorce) when we were destitute and needed help from Social Services, called "Relief" in that era. It was about a five-year span before the situation was resolved. I was sent to live with my father, a decision that was suggested by a very concerned police detective (and it broke my mom's heart). My mother found much better employment, and my sister struck out on her own with a very young daughter and a very difficult move.

My father lived thirty-five miles away in Goshen, a smaller town than Mishawaka, but with better opportunities and friends. Shortly after the heartbreaking move (I was fifteen by then), I was offered a "tryout" in a very popular rock 'n' roll band, *THE DUKES*. The position was for bass guitar, and since I played guitar, the transition was very easy. I became a "one-note man." I started making money, quite a bit of money, and that is when I realized that everyone just needs a little help, an outstretched hand.

Through the rest of my high school years, I flourished. In a California surfing magazine, I saw an ad. A little brown girl with her hand out, tears running down her dusty cheeks. Printed below her picture were the words:

PLEASE HELP HER!
The Christian Children's Fund

She was an orphan in India, living on the streets, and just ten dollars a month would feed her, clothe her, and ensure she had a place to sleep that was safe and warm. How could you beat that? Through a three-year period, I received photos of her growing up, little drawings, and a couple of rudimentary cards in English (the organization was Christian, and taught English at the mission). No one knew that I was participating in this program except my mother, but it gave me inner happiness and a feeling of really being a part of the world.

CHAPTER TWENTY-FOUR

Let's get back to the village in the Amazon. I loved the way Ramon just sat there with a smile on his face, listening. To our surprise, out came the fermented masato. They were offering their precious drink to us, and the moment of truth had arrived. It would have been different if the girls and Joey hadn't seen the process.

Don Ramon
Photo by Patty Webster

Lawrence and I were offered the brewski first, which we, being gentlemen, offered the ladies. I don't think that they had seen this stuff, or even heard about it, for years, probably not since they were young in their village. The two of them put the gourd to their lips, but I do not believe that they drank any. I think that Lawrence did taste it, and Joey, maybe…maybe not. I did drink some, and I liked it. Everyone was smiling and happy.

I noticed that there was a child on the floor playing in a large, cradle-like sheath, which was the protective cover of some type of palm fruit.

She was having a blast with what was available—another example of a people's resilience. You get what you get, and you don't get upset until a different reality sets in, an introduction to: "I want

more than I am able to provide naturally." Then greed and oppression turns into your god.

Women started arriving with bags of crafts. Weavings, carvings, beaded necklaces and bracelets, incredible combs (for the hair), and string bags. They were all constructed with natural jungle fibers and seeds. They laid them out on the floor, and each woman had a "booth." Needless to say, that was the way we could help the most—purchasing the crafts that they had made with their own hands. There was incredible stuff, mediocre stuff, and downright bad stuff. We bought almost all that was available. Nothing like boosting someone's morale.

Ramon in his finest vestments
Photo by Patty Webster

There was one other outlet for their goods: the Dolphin Lady. She brought donated, used clothing from the USA, and traded it to the villages for *artesania* (crafts). When she ran out of clothing she gave them I.O.U. "chits," which they showed us. Some of these had dates a year in the past. The DL had a little store in California that sold the stuff. Is that double dipping?

The Río Tahuayo ran past their village, and at this time of year it was very low, making it hard to bring water up to the village. Ramon told us that the river would start rising very soon when the rains began. Then things would be better.

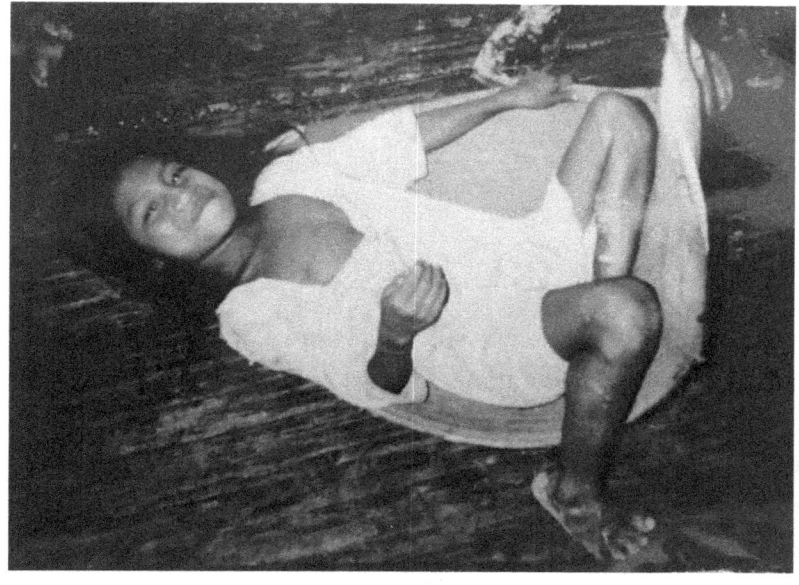

Jivaro girl rocking in a palm sheath

CHAPTER TWENTY-FIVE

Back at Camp One, we laid everything out on the dining tables. We had some nice decorations for our new lodge. We had purchased a couple of *pucunas* (blowguns), colorful *jicaras* (string bags), a few animal carvings made from the local hardwoods, a few really nice baskets woven from the tamshi vine (my favorite), and a ton of stuff that we would never use for anything. There were things we could just place around, like woven frogs, no-shape baskets, etc.

By the way, Vanda's shoes made it through, needing just a little bit of touch-up. When we arrived at camp, she was stylin' again. Joey and the girls were no worse for wear, a day in the jungle hadn't taken a toll on them, so we figured we'd be able to plan just about anything: fishing, swimming, hiking, visiting villages, and playing dominoes, our favorite.

Since we had only our sleeping quarters completed at Camp Two, we still had to cook, eat, shower, and socialize in Camp One. Joey was staying in Camp One full time. The camp had seven bungalows, and all were doubles. From the beginning, the DL was trying to get me together with her young lady helper at the camp. She was not my type, but it was looking like Joey was moving right into position to take up the slack. That was a good thing. We had a week and a half to play, and play we did.

***

The girls wanted to go back to Iquitos midway through the second week. I guess city life is like a drug to people. They complained it was too quiet, not enough to do, and a lot of our time was spent chasing boredom from every nook and cranny. That got boring for me. There was a lot going on with all the fishing, exploring upriver, swimming, trekking, and we did play dominoes, but a large percentage of the action was self-motivated. Nobody really *had* anything to do but me. I conferred with Lawrence continually, but when the rubber hit the road, it was up to me to make it happen.

We had various roundtables with the two brothers, and most talks ended with: "We are not going to be able to do this project without some heavy equipment and a lot of money." Well, there was quite a bit of money, but I think they were talking more about the amount of money they wanted to do the project. As for the heavy equipment they talked about, it would destroy so much jungle just to move it around. These vehicles would need roads to maneuver on, and huge areas to process the fallen trees, etc., etc. We had a much softer and gentler approach in mind. Number one: not cutting trees.

It was still early on when Lawrence realized that things weren't coalescing the way he believed they would, and that the ending would be different than he had envisioned. The two boys would never be able to be left alone to create our dream of a lifetime. It would rapidly turn into their project, a nightmare, and it would change drastically from our vision. We just had to keep them occupied at the camp, and let them have more free time in Iquitos. They still had two weeks of their Peruvian vacation left. Yes, that's right, they were to fly back to Hawaii two weeks after Lawrence, the girls, and Joey left. That would leave me to entertain them. I hoped our shipment from Miami would show up and occupy them with inventory, ha ha ha!

Arriving in Iquitos was always a great thing. Three and a half hours of constant noise, jostling, and water spraying into the boat was a trial, and by the time I finally had to leave Peru in 2002, I had *enjoyed* over a thousand three-and-a-half-hour trips that included breakdowns, towing, and hours of floating. Figuring that in nautical miles, I traveled around the earth four times. Friends here in Florida always ask me to go for outings with them, fishing, sailing, day-drinking excursions, and they cannot understand when I beg-off and state that I have had enough boating for a lifetime (mine).

Another good thing about arriving in Iquitos was Ari's Burger. On our way to the hotel, we stopped by, ate lunch, drank, smoked, and made merry. A great time was had by all. Then it was off to the hotel to make *merrier*.

We only had a few days left, and then almost everyone would leave me. The brothers were going to hang for two more weeks, but everything would fall into place if I could get the shipment out of customs. I would stay in Iquitos, take care of the paperwork, break open the cases, and ensure that everything had arrived. We rented a storeroom for a few months to store everything that would not go to the jungle. The brothers would go through all $75,000 worth of tools and equipment with my list. I wanted to make sure that no one had sticky fingers in Miami, Lima, or Iquitos.

I think the girls finally checked out all the shops in Iquitos and decided that there was really nothing in Iquitos that they wanted. Almost everything was imported from Brazil anyway. By Friday, I was making major inroads to getting our cargo out of customs. We were trying to use the Peruvian law regarding tourism to get the materials and implements that could be imported without paying the 18 percent Importation Tax. With proper paperwork and coima (bribes), our agent was able to speed up the process and it looked like the shipment would be released by Tuesday or Wednesday of the following week. Unfortunately, I had to be with the customs agents through midday, and would miss our last lunch together, which we'd planned to have at the Maloka Restaurant. What a great place, right on the bank of the Amazon River, built in the true Maloka style. Great food too.

Well, I guess I missed more than lunch. Supposedly, from the information I received, my girl and Joey started playing footsie under the table. When I returned to the hotel after dealing with the Peruvian government schmucks all afternoon, Lawrence came to my room.

"Would you mind if Vanda is with Joey tonight since it is his last night in Peru?" he asked. Then he told me of the lunch encounter.

That kind of threw me for a loop, I guess, but I said, "Sure, I don't mind."

Aw man, he was really happy, almost as if saying, "You've had enough of her, share a little." OK.

I had another plan in mind. It was around four in the afternoon, and I was now on a mission. I slowly, but with intent, descended the stairs to the lobby, swaggered over to the reception desk, and waited for the receptionist to turn around and notice me.

"May I help you, Señor Norman?" she asked.

"Well, you may be able to. I am looking for someone to go to dinner with me tonight," I said.

I don't think that she really understood me at first. A quizzical look passed over her face, and she said, "I no understand, what you like?"

"I would like you to go to dinner with me tonight," I said.

She smiled, her face flushed, and she asked, "You want me go to dinner with you?"

"Yes, what time do you finish work?"

"I finish six thirty."

"That is good," I said. "I will be here waiting."

"OK," she said, with a big smile on her face.

That was easy, I guess. I had about two hours to prepare for the date. I went to the corner store, bought a new shirt, walked up to Ari's and ordered a beer. Lawrence walked in and sat down halfway through my beer, and I told him about the evening I'd planned. He thought that was kind of fast, and I told him, "What, I was going to sit around?" I sauntered through the Plaza de Armas and headed back to the hotel to shower again and get ready. I fully figured that Vanda would have moved all her stuff out of our room and into Joey's. Hey, I can roll with it, baby, better than the best. What I encountered was not what I expected.

This deserves an extra line or two: I entered the hotel, asked for my key, and it wasn't there. My receptionist gave me a strange look. I gave a thumbs-up and asked, with an inquisitive look, "Six thirty?"

She looked at me, tentatively, and nodded her head.

What the H was going on? I turned around and saw Lawrence beckoning to me from the couch in the lobby.

What I understood, from what he told me, was that everything was a big misunderstanding. OK, what did that mean?

This is what it meant...

Vanda was up in the room as if nothing had happened. I told Lawrence that I was taking Mira out for dinner at 6:30, because I understood that my time was being cut short and there was a change of partners. It was cool (not that I had ever experienced anything like this in my life). He kind of freaked, but I explained that they were leaving the next day, and I would not be seeing her again, ever. It is what it is. Fuck it, man. I'd never been in this situation before, and I didn't like it.

This mentality did not change the fact that Vanda was in the room, and I would have to deal with her. The last thing I wanted to do was make her feel bad, but at the same time, I really felt like I had been messed with.

Have you ever been asked if the man or woman you were with could be with someone else for the night? It is not a good feeling. It actually had happened to me once before. I did not want to admit it, but I will. My second wife, when we were living in the jungles of Maui, decided she wanted to experience "being with another man." I say what? Luckily, I did prevent it (or maybe I didn't), and finally did end it with her. It was a long ordeal, and what she wanted, she actually achieved in India. Life is not always kind. *Oṃ maṇi padme huṃ.*

Getting back to the story, I turned and went to the elevator. Lawrence followed me and we didn't say a word.

It was getting on to be about five-thirty, and my patience was growing thin. I was over this experience and wanted to move forward.

When I knocked on the door it opened, and Vanda was there, peering into my eyes. I guess she knew that everything had been derailed. Lawrence must have told her, because she had this vulnerable look in her eyes. I walked in and gave her a hug, pointed to myself, and thumbed it toward the door. She looked at me, sadly, and nodded her head. I went in the bathroom, turned on the shower, took off my clothes, and slid in. The next thing I knew, hands were touching my body. I had a woman in the shower with me. It was kind of awkward, but I had to remember, *This girl is here just for the fun.* So, with soap and sponges and other items we had some fun. We are all DOGS, aren't we?

I dressed and readied myself, Vanda telling me that she was just staying in the room and watching TV for the evening. I guess everyone else was going out dancing. I felt a little weird, but…but *nothing*.

DREAM OF A LIFETIME

I was there in the lobby at six thirty. My date was ready, changed into street clothes, and decked out. She looked great, thin, nice hair, and bodacious tatas that made me think, *Carol Dota?* We exchanged air kisses on the cheek and pushed through the doors to the street. I hailed a Motocar and we were off. For every action, there is a reaction.

As I mentioned earlier, the Maloka Restaurant was a local joint, built in the traditional style of corner posts, floor, and thatched roof. In the Amazon Rainforest, it is dark by six o'clock in the evening, being only four degrees south of the equator. Just like our camp in the jungle, the restaurant had open oil lamps on the walkway down to the entrance and all around the perimeter of the eating area. Quite spectacular, and it made for a romantic ambiance, which I was ready for.

Unfortunately, after we ordered drinks, the first information that she stumbled through in broken English was that she had a *novio*, boyfriend, in Lima, and she was getting married in January. It was the end of November and she was out with me. What was she thinking? Then she asked me about the girl in the room. She was probably thinking, *What is he thinking?* Hmm! I tried to explain that she was from Brazil, and she was just here for a vacation.

Mira gave me a strange look and asked, "Not your wife?"

Ahh, great. "No, not my wife, a girl from Rio de Janeiro." I thought that would explain everything, but she gave me a sidelong glance and looked at the menu. Was this a great start or what? At least I didn't have a wife.

It was kind of hard to communicate, as her English vocabulary was mainly for hotel reception, and my Spanish vocabulary was mainly for construction and tools. But we fumbled through the evening, realizing that we did like one another, somewhat. After dinner we walked to the plaza and then on to the hotel. I put her in a Motocar to go home, paid the driver, and entered the lobby.

It was around 9:30 and things were winding down, so I took the elevator up and entered the room with the auxiliary key from reception.

Vanda`had fallen asleep watching HBO, and was under the sheet, curled up on her side. I could see her form through the thin sheet and felt a stirring. I brushed my teeth, disrobed, and slid under the sheet, spooning with her. She stirred and moved her warm, supple body into mine. I could see no reason to resist, and after a few strokes here and there, nature was taking its course. What else can I say? It was our last night, and it was.

- PART XIII -
ALONE IN THE JUNGLE

1993

CHAPTER TWENTY-SIX

The next day, when I took Joey, the girls from Brazil, and my best friend to the airport, I felt emptiness like never before. Full-on interaction from the conception of the project four months earlier, to solitary confinement. Forced labor, money, responsibility, and more employees than I could have imagined a few months earlier. My new life.

The brothers were still with me. Two weeks more of their antics. They wanted to take it as far as possible, including: trying to usurp my authority, changing designs and engineering plans, being devil's advocate, having underage girlfriends, banging up rented motorcycles, and not wanting to do much that was asked of them.

On Wednesday, when I finally received our shipment from the USA, they were saddled with checking each item off of the list and cataloging it. Their work level was about 75 percent, and I continued finding items in boxes months after their departure that had been checked off as "Not Rec'd." I have never been quite sure if it was shoddy work, or intentional.

Oh well, no reason to dwell on this shit. They finally left, and the only real residue left was that sixteen-year-old girl, asking, "Cuando regresara?" (When will he return?)

I had to say, "No se, espero que nunca." (I don't know, hopefully never.)

She cried and went running off, never to be seen again. I hope she wasn't pregnant.

With everyone gone, I was truly alone in Iquitos, in the hotel room, eating meals, buying supplies, traveling to and from the Río Yarapa, and constructing the new lodge. I had lived my wild and reckless years when I was a teen, and again at the end of my twenties, so this was a joy in a lot of ways. I had the notion of keeping a loose journal, and maybe writing a book someday. I was busy from before sunrise until way after sunset every day, and I did want to find someone to spend the weekends with. I was not sitting around moping.

I had decided to build a cargo boat to bring food and supplies to the lodge. This would be much nicer than trying to bring everything from Iquitos into the speedboat every week or two. During the week it could be a river bus and transport the workers. I also wanted to rent a house in town, have an assistant, and go dancing once in a while. After all, this was a land of Salsa, in music and food.

It was December, and Christmas was right around the corner. I had plans to fly to Florida, visit Mom, family, and my two children who were flying in from Oregon. I had to take care of business first. I had a week to set up the work situation in the jungle, give everyone a bit of money for the holidays, return to Iquitos, and fly away.

***

I loved visiting my mom. We always had many items to talk about and discuss. She was working on a new chapbook that she called *Songs from a Bamboo Flute*. Basho was mentioned a few times. This one was all haiku verse. She was very much into Japanese haiku, and the small self-published booklet actually had two or three of her award-winning verses included. Very diverse subject matter.

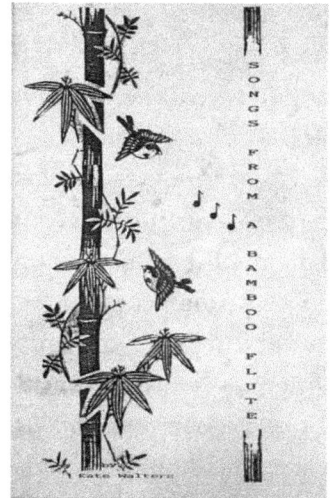

Here are two samples of her haiku, a theme she loved to write about:

Carried on the wind
Listen to the symphony
Of the bamboo flutes

Alone by the stream
Wind-song thru' the bamboo trees
Blends into my dream

I don't believe in giving too much information, thinking that everyone is interested in the smallest details of my life. Sooo, I had a great time with my kids (Luke was nineteen and Star was seventeen), nieces, and nephews. We went to Orlando to visit Disney World, which my kids thought was very fake and stupid. They grew up in Hawaii and were not nurtured on Disney, had gone through our divorce, lived with me, without a mother, for years, and were now trying to make sense of it all, living with their mother in Oregon.

It was a poignant time, a little sullen, and all in all, I was ready to hit the road again. After the tears and goodbyes, off we went to the airport. We went through tears and goodbyes again, and they went west and I went south.

My parting words were:

"Things may not get better. You just learn how to accept, or stuff the things you can't change, change everything that you can, and be damned glad when things go your way. If you are prepared for bad times they are not a shock and you can deal with them. If they never come, then you've dodged the bullet."

They both looked at me, gave a sigh, and one looked up and

to the left, the other looked up to the right, and they walked off through their gate. Another Thing One and Thing Two. By this time it was midday, and there was a really good, really expensive sushi bar in the lobby of the old airport hotel.

The date was January 3, 1993. I figured that this was my last chance to have my favorite food for a while (it ended up being May 20, 1995 when I returned to visit my mom). I ate my fill, relaxed in the lobby for a while, and ambled toward the Faucet Airlines counter.

Federico met me and we chatted a bit about business prospects and his ideas for the travel booking agency we were forming, Eco-Expeditions. It would book all of our passengers and include Cusco, Machu Picchu, and Lake Titicaca. He wanted to make a package deal, "Jungle and Mountains." What a great idea. One week in Cusco, the Inca Trail, and Machu Picchu, then on to the Amazon Rainforest. No one would be able to beat that. He got me on the plane, and four and a half hours later, I was in Iquitos, Peru…home?

CHAPTER TWENTY-SEVEN

The next few months, alone in this very strange land, gave me the opportunity to see and experience *la vida real de la selva*, the real life in the jungle, firsthand. For the first two months the weekends were spent in Iquitos and the jungle, alternately. As our employees multiplied and our food and material needs amplified, I began spending more weekends in the city because we were running out of food and needed construction supplies.

Inadvertently, I began seeing Mira more. This worked into a relationship. I rented a house a few blocks from Ari's and hired, through referrals, a house boy. He lived in the house and guarded it when I was gone. I cooked and ate out when I was in Iquitos, an oddity, and Mira spent most weekends with me. I realized very quickly that the girls in Iquitos liked to play strange mind games. I knew that the "promised man in Lima" was not real, and she was moving toward the idea that I was her new player. We got along OK for about a month, then things started to change. All of a sudden she couldn't come over. Then, when I was in bed and asleep, she would call, saying she could come over. I let that go on for a couple of times, and then just said, "No, don't come over." That didn't go over very well, and I had to go through countless weeping calls in the middle of the night. I held my ground, and I am glad

I did. That was the end of us, and I was alone again. It was OK, though. I had so much work to do I just buried my head and fell into my bed at night. Meanwhile, Mira was trying to work a little magic on me. That didn't work, or maybe it did.

Juan and Norman

Remember Juan, at Ari's, the guy I'd sent out on the river with the wood and cargo boat that sunk? He had become my go-to guy. I mean, this guy was a mover and a shaker like you could not imagine. We were the toxic twins.

What I wanted, he got for me. I was learning more and more Spanish, and made many deals with him. From the Department of Agriculture, Motor Vehicles, banks, the airport, hotels, food venders, boat builders, he knew everyone. If he didn't, he'd tell me how much coima it would take to make it happen.

I did not do anything against the law, I just made everything work faster…very important in a bureaucracy. "I am not a crook." Wait a minute…that sounds way too familiar.

His last and best procurement was *The Girl*. It was March 23, 1993. We were entering Ari's to have lunch. I liked the outside corner table that was shielded from the street. I tried to never have my back to an open area. We sat down. I ordered a beer, Juan a

Juan

Coke, and I rolled one of my special cigs. I was just lighting it, when I looked around the restaurant, and about three tables over I saw two young ladies and a child who were eating. I sort of scanned them from left to right. One girl who had dark hair, one kind of curly haired girl, and one little girl. Drinks came, I took a drag on my cig, and looked over again. As I scanned, because there was a lot of cuteness there, the middle, curly haired girl looked up and we locked eyes. Now I don't know if you have ever seen or felt for yourself, energy pass between two people of opposite sexes. It is like a spark, in Spanish, *chispa*. Sort of knocks you back a little bit. I know she saw and felt it too, because she looked away immediately, blushing. A little while later, she got up and disappeared through a hallway to the bathroom. When she returned, she sat down, facing me. That was good news, we were checking each other out.

I had to think this through. I was going to be here for a few years at least. I was not a person to move from partner to partner; this one was really cute; I was paranoid of STDs; I hated trolling for girls; and I was not into prostitutes. Where did that leave me? My inner voice (not my little head), told me, "Go for it!" As I came to, they were getting up to leave. I looked over and decided.

"Juan, I want to meet that girl, do you know her?"

"Mmm, maybe," he said.

"Follow her and ask if she'll go out with me."

"What do you mean?"

"Tell her that your boss wants to take her out to dinner."

He looked at me kind of weird, and said, "OK." He took off running. He hustled everywhere.

They were halfway across the plaza when he caught up to them. I watched as he stopped them and asked her a question. She didn't respond at first. She looked over at Ari's, looked back at Juan, and said something. Juan looked over and waved to me, motioning for me to come. I got up, told the waitress that I would be right back, and walked across the plaza.

Juan introduced us. "Carmencita, me gustaria presentarte a mi jefe, Norman Walters, y Ella es Carmen Tello." He turned to me and said, "She is related to my wife, distant cousins, and this young lady is her niece, Jezebel." Then, motioning to the child, he said, "This little one is her daughter, Nayla."

She was around three years old and cute as a button, very shy and quiet.

"I asked for her telephone number, she doesn't have one, but she tells me that she lives right in front of you, on Moore Street," he said.

Fate, destiny, karma, whatever you call it, is a debatable issue. Up close, she looked familiar. I couldn't place her, but I definitely knew that I was drawn to her. Carmen explained which house, and Juan seemed to know the location.

"Ask her if she will be home this coming weekend, Juan, and tell her that we will stop by to make plans."

That wasn't so hard. I was a bit anxious when he asked her for her telephone number, but she handled it well, which made me relax. I would find out more later. Right now I had work to do.

Juan and I were in the process of buying all the supplies we would need for the week ahead in the jungle. We were picking up lunch to-go for the boat. Off we went.

Needless to say, or better yet, making a long story short: I courted her for months. We started by going out to eat at different local restaurants, Juan accompanying us for translation (and free food). After two or three times it became ridiculous. I decided to just do it on my own with my trusty little English/Spanish Dictionary and my senses. We included her three-year-old daughter so we could all get acquainted, and ate at La Olla de Oro (The Pot of Gold), the Maloka Restaurant, Ari's, and actually got to know each other a bit. Our communication was getting better. I would look up a word that was the base of the question or statement and say it. Carmen was quick, and was able to put two and two together. Likewise, she would say something and I would look the main word up. We were actually communicating, somewhat.

We started going out dancing on my weekends in Iquitos. Sometimes at night, in clubs, and sometimes Sunday afternoon, at fiestas. We laughed, drank, danced, and had great times, including afternoon river trips in the speedboat *Yacuruna*.

Norman and Carmen

This certainly took away some of the downside of being an ex-pat in a foreign country with very few English speakers. We only had Friday and Saturday nights and sometimes Sundays. In the construction phase of this project, I returned to Iquitos Friday afternoon for supplies, and left for the jungle again on Sunday or Monday morning.

There was only one noteworthy occurrence in all these months. I had a new house boy named Pablo who was living in my house and guarding it while I was away. On weekends, when I was in Iquitos, he would sometimes visit his family. This particular Saturday, in mid-June, he was to go to visit his mom. Carmen and I had gone to dinner, and afterward, to PAX, a small club to dance and have a couple Cuba Libres.

We were feeling on top of the world. We came back to my house and had another little nightcap. She had to go, so I walked her to the door. She stopped, turned to say goodnight, and we embraced, kissed, and kissed and kissed, and all of a sudden, the spark turned to flames. We had kept it under control since the end of March when we started going out. But tonight, we lost all that control. We kept kissing, touching, and the fire was blazing. I clasped her rounded cheeks and pulled her to me.

I didn't hear anything that sounded like NO, mostly just light moans, which I took to mean "yeah baby," so I just kept it going. She had this one-piece outfit that was denim shorts, but like bib-overalls on the top—light blue and white stripes, and she wore a spandex top under it. Needless to say, reaching under her shorts and around her panty edge to enjoy the soft, slick warmth of her was unobstructed. I knew this was going to be the night. We'd been waiting for this.

From the dark room behind us there came a snort and movement on the living room couch. Pablo? He was supposed to be at his mother's house. We stopped everything, so surprised and embarrassed. She ran to the door, opened it, and fled across the street to her house, not looking back. I didn't see her on Sunday before I left. You can bet your ass I got Pablo out of the living room and bought a cot for the storage room. This was not going to happen twice.

***

When I arrived back in Iquitos on Friday, I got all my gear and Motocarred it to my house. As I was getting out of the three-wheeler, I noticed Carmen sitting with her sister in front of her house. I waved and she jumped up and came over. We entered the house, greeted, kissed, and I dropped all my stuff on the floor. I looked at her, and not knowing how to ask her how she felt about what had happened the week before, I shrugged my shoulders, raised my hands palms up, and put a questioning look on my face. She turned red, smiled, and looked away. I showed her the new cot in the storage room and said, "Pablo."

She turned even more red, and smiling, said, "Bueno (good)." I guess that clinched it, and we could look forward to some good times. Yeee-haw!

Now, at the onset, her mom did not want her to get involved with me. I was another gringo, probably had a wife in the USA, just looking for girls, and worthless. Carmen was prohibited from spending the night in my house. "Just look what happened with the last gringo..." She had a three-year-old child and no ring on her finger. What could I possibly offer her? Go figure!

Well, I guess that last night of intimacy really changed things. She spent that night, after dinner and dancing, in my house, and we rolled around in the sheets, literally. The first thing she wanted to do in the morning was get home. Her mom was pissed and threw a fit. Guess what? She stood up to it. We lived together, she learned English, I learned Spanish, got married, built a house, raised little Nayla, had another girl, Stacy, and we have been together since 1993.

Ups and downs, yeah, but still together. Moms aren't *always* right, I guess.

***

Meanwhile, all these trips to the jungle had advanced our project tremendously. We were in June 1993, and the building aspect was coming together. The men were learning the parameters of Norman's Construction, and Norman was learning their jungle building techniques. We were lucky the first winter, for the river did not rise in extremes and we were able to build January through May, in the rainy season.

Esteban at lodge construction

By this time, I had a crew of ninety-six men and women working with me. I had to figure out a

way to get them to work and back home again, without the half hour paddle up, and the half hour paddle down. There was also the problem of at least forty-five to fifty canoes tied up in front of the worksite.

I became more and more interested in the local lore and people. There are only so many personality traits, and many of the workers reminded me of other people I had known in other parts of the world. Like the Macuyama brothers. All four were very competent in everything they were asked to do.

One day, I inquired of Esteban if there were boat builders in the crew. That is when I met the brothers, Manuel, Pancho, Luis, and Miguel. I called them together and asked if they could build me a wooden boat that could hold all the workers, be fast with a small motor, and last for a long time. They all looked at one another, then at Esteban, then at Juan, and they chuckled. I took it to mean that I was asking a lot.

Juan translated for Pancho, "You are asking for all the very best features in one boat. If we can get the wood we want, and the design that we want, we can do it, and you can use a *Peque Peque* (a motor on a gimbal, with a long shaft and a small propeller at the end), or a twenty-five horsepower outboard."

"Well, that sounds like what I want. Give me a list of the materials and you will have them for next week."

We were still borrowing the Dolphin Lady's boats, and I figured, while they were at it, might as well build a couple more boats. I had ninety plus people working, and taking four out to build the boats didn't seem like it would hurt our schedule.

This was really a big thing in the jungle: a ride to work and home again (no more paddling). The commute to Yacumama, for the workers, was twenty to thirty minutes, and the same to return home (jeez, that would be considered good for any metropolitan area in the USA), and they were paddling all the way. Probably not a good comparison, but now I would offer them breakfast and lunch too.

The Macuyama brothers building The Gusano

You can't get much better than that, a ride to work, breakfast and lunch, and a ride home, all on Yacumama. I did finally ask what they had for breakfast before work. You're right, nothing, so that clinched it for me.

The Gusano getting her roof

The boat, when finished, had a green canvas top, and the workers said it looked like a *gusano*, or caterpillar, thus the name.

We had great, good, OK, and borderline passing workers. I tried to mix the questionable workers into all of the groups, but unfortunately, I brought the quality down somewhat. The only thing I could do was change out the worst for new workers. Turns out, most of the worst workers were also the biggest drinkers. This is where my 2" X 10" X 13' tabla (what we call a plank) came in handy.

The Gusano, our river bus

One morning when *The Gusano* docked in Puerto Miguel picking up the workers, the boat was six feet away from the bank. Esteban pushed out the plank and proclaimed, "If you can walk the tabla to the boat, you can come to work. If not, go home and sober up." Fifteen percent did not make it.

After two or three days of not going to work because they could not walk the plank, most of them drank less so they could enter the boat, and their work improved 40–50 percent. The ones who didn't change their habits and could not cross the tabla had to be replaced. Problem solved. Everyone seemed to have higher spirits too. Remember what happened to the poor foreman, Cesar?

We were pushing to open for business in the sunny season, June through October 1994. We had a year to build. In the last eight months, we had progressed considerably: our two houses, the main elevated walkway, fuel dump, tool storage, main lodge, kitchen, and mess hall were pretty much complete.

We could actually sleep, eat, and do our daily duty at the site.

The Main Lodge, 110 miles from the city

Misael, our faithful chef, was very happy he did not have to share with another cook.

Our next big push was to build the segregated bathroom complex, complete with flush toilets, urinals for men and women, showers, and lavatories. These would all feed into a massive underground cesspool system and drain field. No caca in the river for us. There would also be a round hammock house, a laundry room, complete with a heated clothes drying system (I'll tell you about it later). A three-story *taller* (shop) for the solar electric system, and at least seven bungalows for the guests.

It seems like a lot, but ninety construction workers, four kitchen staff, two boat pilots, and two laundry staff can accomplish a lot in a year. The only problem was there was only one person to run everything. Me.

Lawrence came down to Peru as often as he could, and I was very happy for the company, but the visits and the collaborations were too few and far between, and I fear that it did take a toll on me. I was in my early forties, and quite the maniac, so work replaced sanity.

DREAM OF A LIFETIME

In the late summer of '93, Lawrence and Adriana came to the lodge. They stayed for almost a month. Now that we were *couples*, Lawrence and Adriana, Norman and Carmen, things were great.

There were a lot of shared jungle activities, fishing, canoeing, and more fishing, swimming with the piranhas in the black water, eating the piranhas, playing dominoes, music, dancing, and great food. Yeah, baby.

We had two great encounters that summer, both of which turned into lasting friendships as well as incredible business associations.

Lawrence and I loved to sit in the main lodge in the afternoon, smoking, drinking, working on plans and artistic projects. The girls were usually napping before dinner.

One lazy afternoon, we were watching the river pass by when a canoe with two women pulled up to the dock and tied up. Our guard went down to inquire their business, and came back up saying that they wanted to talk to the owners.

Turns out, these two women were starting a medical service group to benefit the villagers. Their mission was to bring doctors, nurses, and clinical aids to our area to set up clinics and treat the maladies and illnesses of the villagers.

Since one of our targeted projects was to set up medical clinics, this seemed to dovetail right into our plans. We talked the afternoon away, and finished up with a price and a date on which we would be ready to receive groups. They were going to go back to the US, work on funding, non-profit status, and administration issues. We were sitting with our sisters in arms.

Patty Webster, RHP, Peru

One of the women, Patty Webster, had been running groups and jungle guiding for one of the area's tour operators for years. She needed a change and ran into an RN, Sadie Brorson, at the right time. They wanted the same thing, and they had everything it would take to get this project off the ground. We were just a check-off on the list. Lol. They were going to name their organization the *Rainforest Health Project.*

Be it noted that RHP assisted and treated the villagers from all the nearby river pueblos in our area for many years. They hosted three, two-week groups a year, and resided at Yacumama until interior problems forced RHP to close.

Being undaunted and the unsinkable vessel that she is, Patty Webster found a way to carry on the promise she had made to the villagers years before. She banded together with known supporters and founded the NGO *Amazon Promise.*

AP picked up where RHP left off, and has provided sustained (recorded) healthcare up to the present date, with their groups still residing at Yacumama Lodge. Amen.

***

Carmen and her daughter, Naylita, started coming out as soon as the lodge was somewhat comfortable. We had some good times, and Carmen loved the hammocks. Nayla made friends with one of the local girls, Kelly, daughter of the Unsung Hero, Samuel (the guy who pulled the motor up from the bowels of the sunken cargo boat). I brought many more loads of wood from Iquitos, and luckily, had no more sunken ships.

One sunny Sunday afternoon at the lodge, I had the bright idea to trek through the jungle, on paths, to visit the chicken farm we had created. We were getting it up and running with more than 300 chickens laying hundreds of eggs a day, donated to the village of Puerto Miguel. "Eggs and chickens for the masses. Let them eat eggs," the Queen screamed. You *know* what I mean. Anyway, one of the staff, Nixon, said he knew the way, about a twenty-plus-minute walk. Great. This was kind of the early days of Carmen's visits, so I didn't have really good outfitting for a three-year-old, but she did have boots. I packed rain gear, a snake bite kit, machete, gun, long sleeved shirts, and off we went with our trusty guide, a local jungle boy.

The trails were a bit ambiguous, and there were a couple of forks that I knew looked suspicious. About ten minutes into our walk, little Nayla couldn't really handle it, so I hefted her up and put her on my shoulders. I could handle that for fifteen minutes more. Then we were twenty minutes in and things did not look familiar. We came up to the edge of a *tahuampa*, or swamp. Carmen slipped, and her boot went into the watery muck. She pulled, and her foot came out of the boot and into the muck, sock and all. Oh boy! I lowered Nayla to the ground and held onto Carmen, pulling her boot out of the mire. She stuck her muddy foot into the boot with tears in her eyes. I asked Nixon if he was lost, and he gave me a deer in the headlights look.

An hour later, we were still walking around. It was actually starting to darken up. I looked at my watch and saw that it was five o'clock. It would be dark by six. Nayla was still on my shoulders, Carmen had fear on her face, and Nixon was totally confused. After another half hour passed, I started creating alternate scenarios. With what I had packed, I could make a tent and we could sleep and survive the night. Not comfortably, but we would survive.

Nixon kept struggling on, and I began hearing the sounds of a boat motor in the distance. Surprisingly, we came upon a property line marker, the ones that I had installed a few months earlier for the Dolphin Camp. These were blue paint on the trees in a line. My God, this would lead to the camp, or deeper into the jungle, depending on which way we turned, left or right. I stood, totally turned around, and decided to follow the line to the left. Nixon was no longer guiding us. As darkness started to crowd in on the trail, I heard the boat motor again, and people yelling. We hurried along, and finally broke through the brush into the top part of the Dolphin Camp. OMG, we were all laughing, and I let Nayla down to walk. As we came up on the Round House, a capybara came up to us and wanted a little attention. Carmen and Nayla petted her, and I could tell they were back with the living.

Carmen and Naylita with capybara

DREAM OF A LIFETIME

We entered the Round House and were offered something to drink. Fresh limeade never tasted so good. About a hundred meters away, I heard *Yacuruna* pull up to the *balsa*, the dock, and a few people running up the wooden walkway. It seems that it had been about two hours since they realized we were lost. That was the sound I'd heard in the distance—my staff trying to find us, up and down the river, calling out our names. I learned a lot that day. Everyone wants to please, and it doesn't matter that they cannot perform or deliver. It only matters that they say, "I can!" I was their guinea pig a few times until I finally said, "I don't think so!"

One time, when Lawrence was visiting, we voiced to Esteban that we wanted to go fishing. It was early afternoon, and the weather was exceptional. We went up the Cumaceba Creek in the *Yacuruna*, threw our lines in close to Carmen Cocha, caught a few fish, went a bit farther upriver, caught some more.

I asked Esteban, "Are there any larger lakes here?"

"Oh yes, it is just a short distance. Do you want to go?"

"Yes, if we can get back before dark," I said.

"It will not be a problem. The lake is just a short distance upriver."

Lawrence said, "Great, let's go."

An hour later, we were still going upriver and I asked, "Hey, are we close to the lake?"

"It is just around the next bend," assured Esteban.

It wasn't around the next bend, or the next, or the next...
I started calculating. Twenty minutes to Carmen Cocha, fifteen minutes of fishing, off to another spot, fifteen minutes, fifteen minutes of fishing, and now, one and a half hours of travel. That meant we'd have about two hours of travel back to Camp One. It was 4:30 p.m.

I explained it to Lawrence, we talked it over a bit, and decided to pull the plug.

"Time to head back to the camp," I yelled over the motor.

"We are almost there," said Esteban.

"BACK TO THE CAMP," I said in my outside voice.

Melanio stopped the boat, confused. I motioned with my up-pointed twirling finger. "Turn it around." He turned around in the small creek and off we went. We arrived in Camp One at 6:30, half an hour after dark. We hadn't brought a light.

If something does not feel right, it probably isn't. Trust your intuition. Our inner voice is always trying to guide us.

CHAPTER TWENTY-EIGHT

We really had an incredible crew. We wanted a round hammock house, but the only way to achieve my design was to create a sixteen-sided structure. I sent the guys into the jungle to find the longest, thickest *shungo* (center post) ever. It took a few days, but one crew came back with shock and awe on their faces, talking of the mother of shungos.

Now mind you, a shungo is the heart of a hardwood tree. It is very dense, and stable. This is what we used for all of our buildings' posts. The trees grow approximately six to twelve inches a year. If the tree is 200 feet tall, it has grown for 200 or 300 years.

The tree had died naturally after living for a hundred years or more, and had lain, rotting, on the jungle floor for a minimum of thirty to fifty years. Some of the larger ones have been there for a hundred years. The heart does not rot, only the woody part and the bark.

We found them by tripping over them, or seeing a hump in the jungle floor. This "mother" was at least forty-five feet of usable shungo, and fourteen inches in diameter. No one had ever seen one like it. It would be the center of my "hexadecagon" hammock house, otherwise known as a sixteen-sided polygon.

Starting the hammock house

This had to be the hardest up-righting of a shungo that these guys had ever encountered. Most of them had never seen a shungo this large, but they did not flinch. I engineered the ropes and the push posts, and everyone understood the concept. We went for it, pushed, pulled, and into the hole it slipped, *ka-chunk*. The framing and the thatching were the next challenges. Whatever I told them I wanted to do, augmented with a sketch, we would do. I admit, they had to re-do a few things here and there, but all in all these guys understood the principles of jungle construction.

I had to pick the right guys for each job. There were divers, climbers, chainsaw operators, mechanics and electricians (few and far between), foremen, boat pilots, cooks, and three or four guys who had the knack for electric tools. These men were basically my sidekicks. I taught them the rudimentary operations of the table saw, the chop saw, circular saw, and electric hand drill. I extended my construction output by three. I was no longer needed for every cut of dimensional lumber. They could still build if I was absent from the site, as long as they had instruction.

The men chosen to construct the roof of the hammock house were fearless. Sure they were roped in, but they were thirty-plus feet off the ground. No fear. That is how I equate everything in my life. Take the proper precautions, and then just go for it.

Raising the shungo

The finished result was nothing less than miraculous and beautiful. They told me that the thatching of the secondary roof was hard. No shit, they had to have skyhooks, which were difficult to find without Google.

VOILA!

CHAPTER TWENTY-NINE

On another fine afternoon, just a few days after the visit from the *Rainforest Health Project* ladies, we watched another canoe come struggling upstream to our dock. Two men paddled up and tied off, and our guard was there to greet them. These men wanted to talk to the owners too.

As luck would have it, these two guys were organizing an expedition company to bring kids to the Amazon. One of them, Jim Cronk, was a middle school teacher who had created the program for eleven- to fourteen-year-olds, along with his partner, Doug Larkin.

The *Children's Environmental Trust (CET)* would bring middle school students to Yacumama Lodge, along with professors from the leading universities in the US, to study every aspect of the Peruvian tropical rainforest.

WOW! We were again sitting with our brothers in arms. What a great time we had (they liked beer). We worked out

James Cronk, CET

a basic plan, tentative prices and dates, numbers and timeline. These people were stellar. We were just enjoying the afternoon, groovin' two times, and now we would have tentative groups for 1995.

We enjoyed the CET groups for many years, hosting hundreds of young people, helping them to understand the importance of animals and trees and clean water in our world, and many researching professors, passing sabbaticals at Yacumama Lodge, studying the flora and fauna.

Unfortunately, in our world, good things do come to an end (more often than bad things), and we all lost the benefits of the *Children's Environmental Trust* at the turn of the century. Life goes on, c'est la vie, and Jim and I are still tight.

***

I would call that summer of '93 very satisfying personally, business-wise, in construction advancement, community involvement, and in sexual and social interaction with our partners. It couldn't get much better.

But as I said, all good things come to an end.

Ours was coming to an end. Adriana was returning to Brazil, Lawrence was going back to the States, Carmen and I would remain. At least I wasn't going to be left alone this time. Being a stranger in a strange land can wear on a body.

We all decided to go to Lima for our big bang goodbye. We stayed in the Las Americas Hotel. Everyone but Carmen was under the weather. I had walking pneumonia, Lawrence and Adriana had jungle rashes. Isn't life wonderful?

It was my first time in Lima, and Carmen hadn't been since childhood. We had a blast.

Lima, Peru is international/metropolitan, so we had amenities that I hadn't seen in a year. Jacuzzi, real hotel room service, cinema (with new movies), espresso café and toasted croissants and baguette in the mornings.

I was saying before that it couldn't get much better...well, it did. I got two big injections in my butt cheeks, recovered from pneumonia, and Carmen made an ointment from ingredients in the *farmacia* and Lawrence and Adriana overcame their rashes, all in the luxurious environment of the hotel.

– PART XIV –
THE SECOND YEAR

CHAPTER THIRTY

In my second year, 1994, the water rose to a record high. The peak water level usually occurred around March or April. By February, the river had risen to one foot below the dark water-stained marks on the trees. All the men were surprised that I had decided to situate the floors one meter above the mark. I mean, that mark was the highest the river had ever gotten in their entire lifetime. Safe? I would say so.

It turned out to be a good decision, because that year the river rose to eighteen inches *above* the marks. Unfortunately, in the years since (with El Niño and global warming), the river has risen above our floors quite a few times. A grand cleaning job was had by all. I even raised all the *new* re-construction floors (in 2008, after the arson fire) another half meter, but with all the woes of our climate change in the last few years (twenty-plus years later), the river has risen above even the new construction.

There was one little boy, the son of one of our employees, who loved the high water.

Rodmer in the flood

He would paddle out in the river and play around. Good balance. I drew him in 1999.

One day in January or February of 1994, I was with a group of workers, following a group of scout canoes. At this time the rivers were connected, river to river to river, ad infinitum. No land at all. We were sloshing through muddy water, up to mid-chest, machetes over our heads, looking for tamshi, leaf, and wood. We needed just a few materials to complete a project.

It was a day to be remembered after days of rain and gloom. The sun had come out and the sky was blue. We were slowly moving through an open area, trees all around, when I noticed a big, fat tube in the lower branches of a tree. The tree was about thirty feet from our search party, and I suddenly realized that the "tube" was a snake. I pointed at it, and Esteban nodded his head a couple of times. He nudged me with his elbow and said, "They only eat gringos!" He smiled at me and then laughed.

The boa was probably twenty to twenty-five feet long, and sixteen to eighteen inches in diameter. It appeared to be sunning itself in the lower branches, and as we were passing, it started slithering down the tree. It moved faster than I would have expected, and was already entering the nearby water.

It was truly able to consume one of us, or it would at least be a ferocious battle. As its tail tip entered the water, we just watched to see which way it was going since we were almost fifty feet from the tree. The next seconds dragged on until one of the closest guys pointed and yelled, "Es por alla!" ("It's over there!")

Everyone whooped it up. No one had a gun because of the water, so it would have been a fight to the finish with machetes. But we dodged the bullet and were on our way again.

The poisonous snakes living in the Amazon are to be respected and feared. Most are of the viper variety. Some, like the bushmaster, the famous fer-de-lance, tropical rattlesnake, and coral snake, are the most feared. You die from these if you don't get treatment quickly.

During our four years building Yacumama Lodge, there were deaths and countless snakebites, but the one that affected me the most was the Puerto Miguel resident who went upriver (in canoes), hunting, with his two sons. A week hunting trip, two full days paddling upstream, three days hunting and fishing, and one and a half days paddling downstream. The normal trip. Food for the family. He'd done it many times. They fared well and were on their way back home and more than halfway there. They stopped to sleep for the night and he built their campsite on the bank while his two sons went to collect *ramas*, branches, to burn. He heard his ten-year-old scream and ran to find him. He was lying on the ground, clutching his leg. There was a dead *shushupe*, bushmaster, with its head cut off, squirming next to him. His son had killed it. He grabbed the young boy and ran for the canoes. The eight-year-old was already preparing the canoes, and they left their sleeping gear on the bank, jumped in the canoes, and hit it downstream. He was twenty minutes closer to Yacumama than the village, and we had fast speedboats to reach Nauta, the closest clinic. Possibly there was a chance. They paddled at full speed, not thinking of exhaustion, for hours and hours.

I was summoned from the *comedor*, dining room, at 5:00 a.m. while drinking my coffee. I hurried to the dock and found the father, Jose, holding his son. I felt the boy's neck and pronounced him dead. Supposedly, eight hours was the limit to survive a shushupe bite. If he camped at ten o'clock the night before, he had been at least nine and a half hours from Yacumama and possible salvation.

The men of the villages are a stoic lot, and he

was in shock. I told him not to worry, we would help him bury his son, and that I would make a nice coffin for him. I knew the boy, and almost all 250 inhabitants of Puerto Miguel and their families within the first year.

***

We had built like madmen through 1993 — the common area and dining room, kitchen, hammock house, bathrooms, septic tanks and drain fields, employee areas, dishwashing, storage, bungalows — and now it was 1994, time for the solar tower, employee dining, laundry with wood stove heated drying room, and a large dock for boats and fishing. We were busy, and all standard building materials had to come from Iquitos. Logistics were a nightmare that I kept having week, after week, after week.

We finally built our cargo boat, *Yacumama II*, and it was a Godsend. I am talkin' tons and tons of food, supplies, gas, kerosene, people, and whatever, every week. It was an eighteen- to twenty-hour trip, lodge to Iquitos, Iquitos to lodge. It was worth every penny.

CHAPTER THIRTY-ONE

Mortality is an accepted reality in the jungle. People die young, middle aged, old, and as infants. At funerals, women wail and keen, men smoke, drink, and play casino all night. I have been to a few, mostly drownings of toddlers, old fishermen, and drunks. Most happen in the wet season, due to flooding. We built most of the caskets for the village.

We learned that there are no secrets in the jungle. When anything changes, like beatings, break-ups, new inhabitants, any change at all, everyone knows.

Well...a new inhabitant arrived to stay in Puerto Miguel. He was kind of a mystery, late twenties, thin, spoke mainly German, a bit of Spanish, and spent most of his time in Julio's Cantina.

The next that I heard, he had hooked up with one of the local girls. I knew her father, Don Antonio. He was one of our employees, and he wasn't very pleased with the situation. The young German man had (sort of) talked his way into living at Don Antonio's house. He had some money and was flashing it around like the white touristy people do in the jungle villages. Trolling.

A few weeks later, on Friday, midday, the whole family (with the young man) paddled by Yacumama Lodge in two canoes. We exchanged waves, and I figured they were going on a hunting/

fishing weekend trip. I went into Iquitos for the weekend to see my family, buy supplies, and do my end-of-week business.

Returning Monday afternoon, all was well, *tranquilo*. I fished in the late afternoon, caught a few mota catfish, and dined like a king.

This was 1993, and I was just starting to record my Amazon adventure experiences. At Christmastime, I brought an old portable Royal typewriter with me. I typed into the night to fight boredom, as well as to record my adventure. I lost interest in a couple of years, and filed the twenty-seven (legal size, single spaced) page, five-chapter account. I was just living, being, and experiencing life after that.

***

Tuesday, mid-morning, I was directing the troops when Esteban came running up.

"Señor, come to the dock, the German is dead!"

"What do you mean, *dead*?" I asked.

"He's been shot!"

I hurried to the dock, and lo and behold, there was the German in one of the canoes, his hands up by his chest and a ragged, bloody hole in his sternum. He was stiff with rigor mortis and had a surprised look on his anguished face. His eyes were still open, fogged over and dry looking. I really did not have to check for a pulse, but I did...yup, gone. I closed his eyelids the best I could, and called for a couple of sheets to wrap him in.

"Esteban, ask them what happened," I said.

"Don Antonio, que paso?"

"El se disparo a si mismo," answered Antonio.

I looked at the family. The girl looked like she had been crying, but everyone else just stood there, nodding their heads yes. He committed suicide?

Antonio said they wanted to take him to Puerto Miguel to clean him up and get him ready for burial. Hmm... I told everyone to just relax a minute, and I went into my office and radioed the police in Yucuruchi, a depot on the Ucayali River, a good two to three hours from the lodge by land and water.

I advised them that the foreign man was dead, shot by a shotgun at very close range, and we needed them to come to Puerto Miguel to investigate. The police would be there in the morning if I would give them gasoline for their boat. That was totally normal for the jungle. If we needed or wanted help from the authorities, we had to pay their way, so I complied.

The women of the pueblo wanted to have a wake for him that night, and I agreed to transport the body to Iquitos the next day after my office contacted the German representative in Iquitos.

I advised the family that the Yucuruchi Police would be there in the morning, and gave them the gasoline for the PO-PO, making sure they understood me, "Para la policía!"

I mulled over all of the facts, over and over, and came up with the same scenario each time. The way his hands were grasping his chest, the surprised look on his face, and the single load, long barrel, twelve-gauge shotgun, would make it very difficult, if not impossible, for him to have pointed it at his heart, and subsequently reach the trigger and discharge the rifle. Something just didn't smell right, but I would wait for the police report. Maybe I was just Kojak-ing out. That evening we made a wood box for transport of the body to Iquitos.

***

The next day when I reached Puerto Miguel, I found everything all wrapped up, literally. The police were finished with their investigation, deemed suicide, they took the gasoline and all of his personal items that were on his person, as well as in Antonio's house. I asked Antonio why he had given the police the German's passport, visa, money, and clothes.

"Porque la polícia quireia todo," he replied. "Y yo no quiero problemas con la polícia."

The police wanted everything, and he didn't want problems? Holy shit, he might have just killed a foreign tourist and he was worried about that?

I saw why when I looked at the wrapped body. He was lying flat with his arms at his sides. I saw no indication of the wrap being opened, and I saw no tears. I asked Antonio just what the police took. I guess *everything* was his military boots, all his expedition clothes, his money (yes, I remembered the talk of the town, the roll of cash), passport, visa, wallet, aviator sunglasses, and tennis shoes.

OK, I had to have his documents and possessions to turn over to the German representative in Iquitos with the body. We were going to have to go to Yucuruchi to demand the German's possessions. It would be about three hours out of our way, but a necessary trip. We loaded the poor guy into the casket, tacked down the lid, and sped off down the Río Yarapa.

I started putting the pieces of the puzzle together, en route. It looked to me like they got rid of the German, who was a questionable addition to the community, stole his money, clothes, shoes, backpack, and I was wagering that when we got to Yucuruchi I would be in for another surprise.

***

When we reached the police depot, there was no one manning the office and it was locked. I remembered where Jose the policeman lived, so we trudged through the muddy path to his house, getting our ration of chiggers for the day (not my favorite little pest).

"Buenas tardes, Señor Norman, que sorpresa," exclaimed Jose. "Que te trae por aquí?"

Yes, I bet it was a surprise. I interrupted his four-hour lunch siesta, *sorry*! So I explained why I was in Yucuruchi, how I had found no trace of an investigation, none of the German's possessions, no documents or money, and that the villagers said that he took them all.

Jose gave me a surprised look, and told me he had brought just his wallet with identification, passport, and visa back to Yucuruchi. There was no more. Antonio had told him that they left everything on the riverbank, hurrying to try to "save him."

Umm, he had been shot in the heart.

I told Jose that I was transporting the body to Iquitos, and I needed his documents and wallet identification for the German consul.

"Ohh, no, Señor Norman, lo necesito para mi informe, y su identificación," stammered Jose. He needed everything to ID the body and write his report.

"Muy bien," I said. "Voy a dejar su cadáver contigo también." I'd just leave him the corpse, too!

He looked in my eyes, and realized that I was not joking and that the charade was over.

"Dame un documento para firmar, para sus documentos de identidad, y pasaporte," I stated. "Entonces me iré y no te causare ningún problema." (Give me a paper to sign for his ID and passport, and I will leave and cause you no trouble.)

He sat there, contemplating for a minute or so, looked up, and avoiding my eyes, said, "Muy bien, Señor Norman!"

He turned to his typewriter and painstakingly typed out a letter of deliverance, carbon copied. I had the German's ID, signed, sealed, and delivered.

Back in the boat, speeding down the Río Ucayali, I opened his wallet, and to my surprise, he was older than I had thought. He had an East Berlin identification card that stated he was a Stasi agent from East Germany and forty years old. That card identified him as a secret police infiltrator. Maybe not now, since we were in the year 1994, but not too many years prior, either, since the Berlin Wall was torn down in 1989. I still remember old Ronnie ordering, "Mr. Gorbachev, open this gate. Mr. Gorbachev, tear down this wall!"

That was in 1987, and it took two years for Mikhail to comply, but he did it.

I realized that I might be in over my head, so I decided to have my office call the German consul and have him meet me at a very obscure dock in Iquitos to deliver the body.

A mile away from the dock, I was able to see that there were at least 200 people there. Vans from the local radio and television stations were parked, and it looked like a disaster to me. We pulled in very slowly, looking for the least populated point to meet my contact and deliver the coffin.

I guess it really didn't matter, because we were all filmed and the whole account was public. A van was waiting for the coffin, and I delivered the document from Yucuruchi and all of the identification papers, wallet, passport, and visa to the German consul.

He asked me about the possessions, and I told him that what I gave him was all that the authorities had given me. He didn't appear to be very happy, possibly because he wanted the money also. I really do not know, but as I climbed the stairs to the street, the television station reporter stuck the microphone in my face and asked me questions. I ignored him and hailed a Motocar, and as we sped off, I tried to decompress. What a trip!

- PART XV -
GOSHEN, INDIANA

Buddy Makes It "Big"
Late 1969-1970

CHAPTER THIRTY-TWO

Our second hitchhiking odyssey was over, and Larry's parents were very nice about our unexpected arrival, even offering me a bedroom to stay in for a while. This surprised me, since there was a bit of bad blood between us, seeing as how I'd lured their inexperienced son to Sin City! Hey, he wanted to go.

Larry's dad was a head professor at the local Mennonite college, and he was able to get us jobs preparing the food for the students. That was cool. I don't remember what Larry did, probably the same thing as me, but I remember it was pretty grueling. Grilling hundreds of steaks, or hamburgers, or hotdogs, deep frying fish sticks and French fries, a hundred gallons of mashed potatoes, macaroni, and spaghetti. Boy, I hadn't worked like that since I was the sole attendant at a truck stop in Van Wert, Ohio, pumping gas, washing windshields, being the waiter, short-order cook, server, busser, dishwasher, and cashier. You can believe that…or don't!

I even shoveled out a sheep shed in May once, to get it ready for the next season. You have any idea how much sheep shit accumulates over the winter in a closed sheep shed with two feet of snow outside for six months? A lot! And the smell is so refreshing.

Boring? For me too. All I can say is that this went on for a while, with Larry making silk screened T-shirts to sell, and I was getting back into my art and music, slowly. I played some music, bought a Martin D-28 from Rex at his Record Rack, and completed a few etchings, but life seemed to get stagnant. I decided to create an art colony. I talked with the most radical of my friends and found that there was the beginning of one already started. I was able to rent a room as a studio, and was free to create whatever I desired, even havoc.

It was called Brunies North, which I understand, thanks to my friend Mike G., originated in the Gunter Grass novel *Dog Years*. Jenny Brunies was a character in the book. Lee H. and friends were inspired to create a Brunies South at IU, Bloomington. All of my Bohemian friends, not hippies, but alternative people, those who had never found their place in society, gathered together.

You know what they say, "Where two or more are gathered in my name..."

Sure, it was a dead-end destination, but we made the best of it. I was turned off to drugs from what had happened in NYC, but still needed an escape. I turned to alcohol, like some of us did. What a great time. I developed an artistic technique that I called "turpentine wash," a heavy graphite and wispy pastel rendering. I did mainly realistic portraits of my artistic idols like Modigliani, Steichen, and Stieglitz, blended together with a wash of turpentine. I used this vehicle because it is processed from the pine tree, and I was becoming Mr. Natural. I kept my turpentine in a used beer can...the easiest way to use it. I also drank beer out of beer cans. I remember being totally caught up in the moment, graphite dust, pastels in the air, and the smell of turpentine enveloping me as I created another one of my artistic escapes. I grabbed for my beer and chugged... Holy shit, wrong can. UGH!

Did you know that in the earlier centuries, turpentine was ingested for the riddance of parasites in the human digestive system? Pine tree sap. *"What, me worry?"*

We had Nomadic weekend outings to the beaches of Lake Michigan with food, beer, wine, music, swimming, occasional coupling, and the best existential discussions you could ever imagine.

I believe we were all living the dream, how it must have been in Paris, New York, and Amsterdam. Wild and romantic, rebellious and free, in the late nineteenth and early twentieth centuries.

Michael F., Mike G., Gulinora, Dave, Tom, Lee, Lee's sister, Me, Michael C.

Michael F., an incredible pianist, and I, with excess time on our hands (idle hands, you know what they say?) decided to write a porno book about high school. They were very risqué in the sixties. Our idea was to write a book that was very tongue-in-cheek funny, and a big spoof on these books that in this time, were very slimy.

Deliberating on the title over petite glasses of Bénédictine, we decided on: **BUDDY MAKES IT "BIG"**

We pulled out our dueling typewriters, sat facing each other at the kitchen table (*No matter where I serve my guests, it seems they like my kitchen best!*), and began typing and drinking. Chapter One, line one: **"Buddy woke up with a rod!"**

A little-known fact (maybe) that not too many people are aware of, is that in the very early seventeenth century, King James decided to translate the ancient Latin, Greek, and Hebrew religious texts into *The English Bible King James Version*. Started in 1604, completed and printed in 1611, it became the talk of the town.

I can't help thinking that, after the Spanish Inquisition and the Crusades, power and fear were more important than truth. A monk's life was probably somewhat boring, so hey, drink wine and Bénédictine (created by a monk in 1510), and translate the Bible the way you want it to be. Great idea, right?

If the monks could do it, then so could we. Michael could type like 105 wpm with three errors. I could type about thirty-five wpm with ten errors. I mean, I was a guitarist, and dexterous, but Michael...he was a virtuoso.

Typing, collaborating, drinking, and laughing, we created a masterpiece that no publisher would want because it was funny, not slimy. Today it would probably be published. I do believe that Michael still has the original manuscript. Hmm, not a bad idea.

Well, everything got kind of hazy after a while, being the same old, same old, and I decided to change scenery. Larry and I decided to hitchhike to California. Our friend Thayer from the Central Park encounter was there, and we figured 'ol Cal was a great place to spend the winter. It was only 2,500 miles away, a cinch.

– PART XVI –
WILD PARTY ON THE RÍO YARAPA

1994

CHAPTER THIRTY-THREE

One afternoon while I was calculating my designs for the wood heated clothes dryer, Esteban came quietly up to say, "Señor

Norman, we are invited to a party at the Pacaya family's house tonight. The invitation is for all the staff of Yacumama. It is the birthday of Beltran, the most famous artist in Puerto Miguel, and your friend."

Beltran Pacaya was an incredible artist, painter, sculptor, and a legend among his people. He had polio from birth. His legs did not develop normally, and were unusable. He had to be carried (the villagers called him "Backpack," you can imagine why), and didn't achieve mobility until he acquired a wheelchair much later.

After dinner, all the staff not critical to security loaded into the *Yacuruna,* and we took off for the *casa de Pacaya*, their house.

Darkness was dropping its veil as we pulled up to the house, and I could see that quite a few peeps were already there. It was during the time of high-water flooding, so we were able to tie up on the veranda railing. The house was the maloka style, and the floor was approximately five feet above the actual ground. Puerto Miguel was flooded, and all was water, río to río to río, river to river to river.

When this flooding happens (not every year, but some years) between December and May, the villagers' fields of rice and yuca are covered and lost, their chickens live in their tambo houses, and they have to raise their floors or live, sleep, and eat in water.

The worst flood in recorded history came in 1994. The river rose eighteen inches above the dark water marks on the trees. Our floors at the lodge were above water only because I had built them over a meter above the water marks on the trees.

The only food for the villagers consisted of fish, whatever dry goods that they were able to salvage, fish, Yuca that they were able to dig up before the water engulfed their fields, fish, and more fish.

Río to Río to Río to Río

I decided to pack the *Yacumama II*, our cargo boat, with rice, oil, salt, potatoes, and a few other foodstuffs (about three tons) in Iquitos, motor up river to our area and deliver food to over 150 families (personally). The worst affected in our area were the villages of Puerto Miguel and Libertad. We also brought *pan bico* for the kids, which were small, torpedo-shaped breads that they all loved.

Where was I? Oh yeah, the party on the river...

We disembarked and were welcomed by a crowd of friends and the Pacaya family. Beltran was playing guitar. I forgot to tell you that he was also a guitarist/singer. I noticed that the water was just below the floorboards of the tambo house. Good thing the water would start going down in about a month or so, because it put a lot of stress and anxiety on the villagers.

Julio's Bodega was right next door, so there was no problem getting cases of cold beer and bottles of aguardiente.

Julio also rented his sound system to the Pacayas, and later, there would be blaring music like you couldn't imagine. My favorite in those days was Mana. I couldn't believe such a civilized rock and roll sound could be achieved in the Latino culture.

Why, I loved it so much, that I chose "Oye Mi Amor," by Mana as my wedding song to Carmen in 1996.

As the night ground on, more and more people arrived in various states of sobriety. The Pacayas had two tambo-style houses side by side, with a gutter between them to catch the rain water. We had to jump across a two-foot gap to get the cold beer. No problemo! (Even though there was five feet of water below that gap.)

Now, let me give you a heads-up: The four big posts that were the corner supports for all the rigidity and stability of the house, were sunk about a meter or so into the clay soil. Just keep in mind, that there had been three to five feet of water around the posts for three months. There were more than fifty party hearty friends, dancing, moving to and fro, gyrating around, and having a very good time.

Melanio was sitting in the *Yacuruna*, watching everyone getting loaded and diffusing the BS of everyday jungle life. He might have been dozing a bit, seeing as how it was almost midnight. I thought it was time for another beer, and maybe a shot of Clavo huasca, my favorite jungle juice.

I walked toward the kitchen tambo and started to jump across the opening. I landed in...WATER? Yeah, water. I was up to my neck in water.

This was really weird. Up to my neck in water three times in one year. The first time was with the employees, gathering building materials. Remember the thirty-foot serpent sunning in the tree? The second was just about two months before this rescue, when I was drinking my Clavo huasca and having a good time shootin' the shit at Poncho's bar. *Yacuruna* was tied up to a small floating *balsa*, or dock, and the water was up to the floorboards of the bar.

Around midnight I'd had enough and decided that it was time to return home to the lodge. It was very dark (no electricity in Puerto Miguel), and as I stepped off the veranda, I quickly assessed that there was no balsa, just water. As I was sinking, I thought about my new leather tennis shoes I was wearing.

There I was, climbing up the porch railing, everyone laughing, and the joke was on me. HA, HA, HA, they'd moved the balsa. What a bunch of kidders, God love 'em.

Back to reality and my third situation. I quickly realized that one of the buildings had moved. Pulling myself up to the kitchen tambo, I surmised that the main building, where all the people were dancing, was moving away from me, very slowly, but moving.

I yelled for Melanio, but I don't think he heard me with all the loud music. I always carried a small Maglite in my pocket, so I shined it at the boat and caught his attention. I blinked it a few times and heard the low, rumbling sound of *Yacuruna* coming alive. The boat was by my side in a few seconds, and we took off toward the side of the house that was entering the water.

By this time, the more astute villagers were noticing that the floor was getting a bit unlevel. We pulled around to the bad side of the house, tied off, and pointed the bow of the boat against the floorboards. I motioned to Melanio to hit the throttle. I was trying to keep the house from going all the way over while I got the old folks and the young folks in the boat. The adults could just jump off and swim, which they were doing.

I was saturated and dripping, but I told Esteban to round up our employees and get the *viejos*, old folks, and the *chiquillas*, little kids, in the boat. Man alive, everyone was scrambling, except the ones we were evacuating. The viejos and the infants couldn't even walk, run, or swim to escape.

Yacuruna was doing an incredible job of counteracting the fall of the tambo, but there was this thing called gravity involved, and it was still going down, just more slowly. Believe it or not, with the house empty, *Yacuruna* down to the gunwales, and more than thirty peeps (infants, toddlers, mamas, and viejos) in the boat, I untied it and we pulled away. Far away.

Remember that our supplies had arrived from the US a while back, and I was in possession of our *one million candle power spotlight*. I shined it on the house, and we all watched as it crashed, twisting, screeching, and wrenching, into the water, extinguishing the *macheros*, kerosene lamps, one by one. We unloaded all the villagers to the bodega next door, consoled the Pacaya family, said our goodbyes, and took off upriver to the lodge.

Now we knew why we named the boat *Yacuruna*, "Father of the Water." The protector of family. Not one drowning, not one death.

CHAPTER THIRTY-FOUR

Article by Charlie and
Felicia Cowden

One of the most incredible obstacles that we surmounted in 1994, was bringing solar power to the jungle. Charlie (solar tech), and Felicia (photographer), neighbors of Lawrence on Kauai, were brought to Yacumama for the installation of our solar power system.

Who turned on the lights in the jungle? WE DID!

It was not an easy job, but we did have an enjoyable time. Lawrence and Adriana wanted to be at the lodge for the installation, and he brought his two daughters from Hawaii. My two kids arrived from Oregon, so we fished, swam, played dominoes, listened to music, and reunited after years of living different lives. The kids were all in their mid-teens at that time, and hadn't seen each other since they were very young, playing naked on the beach.

Our batteries had been stored for a year on a concrete floor. Duh, *ruined*! Heavier cable had to be purchased to run the current to our distant kitchen and meeting area. The system was 120V, and

Peru has 240V. That meant light bulbs from the US. Good thing Charlie brought some bulbs with him.

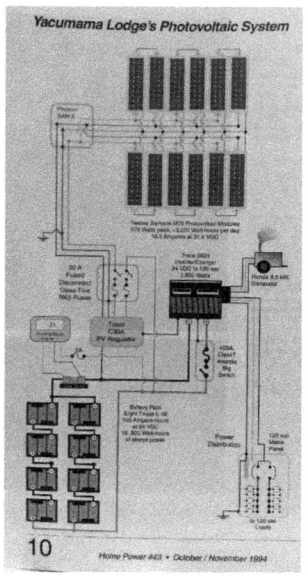

But…lights changed everything. We had better breakfast and dinner prep, night dishwashing, playing dominoes at night, conversing, and playing *Sapo*. This is the greatest game I have ever played, found mainly in bars where the patrons play for beers. It consists of a cabinet with incredible chutes and passages incorporated inside. There is a leather-covered top with various holes cut through coinciding with the chutes. There is also a large, open-mouthed brass toad called a Sapo straddling one of the holes, and three spinning, brass paddle wheels on three of the others. You throw heavy brass coins at the Sapo's mouth and the holes in the top, and if they enter, the coins slide down the chutes to numbered pigeon holes for your score. Great competition.

Above: A view of part of Yacumama Lodge from the tower that holds the photovoltaic modules

I had been living by kerosene lamps and a few Aladdin lamps for a year or more. It felt good being back in the twentieth century.

Charlie and Felicia, thanks to you two!

CHAPTER THIRTY-FIVE

After the solar installation, we all went to Cusco and Machu Picchu. June is winter in Peru. Cusco, at 10,000 feet above sea level, was very cold. We had just arrived from the steamy jungle and were not prepared at all.

Arriving at the Cusco airport, there were countless venders selling coca leaves with an alkaline substance, rolled into a ball called *cal* (lime in English). You masticate the leaves and scrape the cal into your mouth with your teeth, mix it with the chewed leaves, and they say it helps with altitude sickness. It also really numbs your whole mouth.

This process has been used by the high altitude inhabitants of South America since the Inca times or before. It was a pretty cool experience, but just one of many on this bittersweet tour of culture.

We had brought sweaters and jackets, but nothing to protect head, neck, and hands at twenty-eight degrees F. Carmen and Adriana were the only ones in the group never to have seen snow or feel the type of cold bestowed upon us.

Federico (remember him), our Miami, FL agency manager, had made all of our reservations and sent Lawrence the vouchers. We were to be on a first-class vacation at the Royal Inca Hotel, tours, train rides to Machu Picchu and back, hotel at the actual ruins site, guided tours of all the sights, and the best restaurants. It couldn't get much better, you know, to impress our two girlfriends and our kids. The good life.

Peru, at this time, was in the first stages of recuperation from the Shining Path's terrorism (which still existed, but was being extinguished by the Fujimori government). Tourism was just starting to come back, hotels were remodeling, tourist dollars were returning, slowly.

The taxi dropped us off at the hotel, and when we finally got checked in (we were not on the reservation list, but somehow we were able to get rooms), I decided that we needed to be better prepared for the cold. I asked if there was a store nearby where we could buy gloves, scarves, and hats. The receptionist told me that there should be venders outside the hotel on the street, and there were.

We bought everything we needed, 100 percent wool. On one of our city tours, we even bought serapes. We were set and ready to go.

At this point, rather than playing the violin, I am just going to run through the comedy of errors we encountered for the next few days.

The train left at 7:00 a.m., and we had to check in at 5:00 a.m. to secure our seats. We didn't have enough tickets, and had to buy more, but the seating was numbered so we were all in different cars.

We arrived at the bus stop in Aguas Calientes (the base town for the tour to Machu Picchu) at around 10:00 a.m. The bus ride was about forty-five minutes on a very dangerous, one-and-a-half lane switchback road where something incredible occurred: At the bottom of the mountain, on the road, a small boy, maybe eight years old, stood waving at us very dramatically. We all waved back. How cute. Each switchback took about eight minutes, and when we were around the first curve and on the upward grade, there stood the boy. We all marveled at it, and I noticed that there was a trail opening at each side of the road. Did that really mean that the boy just ran uphill, around 200 feet, to meet us? As we passed by, he yelled, "Heeelloooooooo!"

That was very impressive, and what was even more impressive, was that he was at every upward grade, all the way to the top. At about the fourth round, everyone started throwing money out the windows at him.

From the hotel bus stop we could see the ruins, but it was lunchtime and the teens were hungry. We had to check-in and find our guide. I was looking around when I noticed the boy jump into the empty bus for a ride down the mountain. Smart kid!

Lawrence and I ordered and paid for food for everyone. While we were waiting, we saw a guy with a placard with "BISHOP" written on it. Hey, must be our guide.

"My name is Carlos, and I will be your guide for today," he said, introducing himself.

"Let the girls and the kids keep eating, and we can go to check-in," I said to Lawrence. "Carlos can help us."

Of course, there was a line at reception so we waited and waited. I checked on the family a couple of times and returned to the desk. We decided to let Carlos take the family on a tour while we checked in. *How hard could it be?* I walked Carlos down to the lunch area and explained the situation to everyone. Great plan.

Off they went, and I hustled up to the desk line. We were next. The receptionist spoke our language, so Lawrence gave her the vouchers and smiled. She looked on the computer, an old, old IBM computer. She couldn't find us.

"Please check again," he pleaded. "We must be there, and we have the vouchers."

"I'm sorry, sir, but I cannot find the voucher numbers. Let me call my manager," she answered with a frown.

We looked at each other and had the same thought: *That's how hard it can be.* While we waited for the manager, I decided to run down and get Carlos. "Help us, Obi Wan Kenobi, you're our only hope."

When we got back, the manager invited us into his office. He had a phone and Lawrence asked if he could use it to call our agent in the US. He couldn't call the US on the phone. It was only for national calls, but he would call the tour company and investigate. We could wait outside, and he would call us.

Twenty minutes later, he opened the door and asked us to return.

"I'm sorry, but it appears that the tour company has made an error, and the hotel is full. Every room has checked in. I'm sorry, there is nothing I can do." He got up from his desk and ushered us out.

OK, Plan B. What was Plan B? Carlos said that he could make a call from the pay phone... PAY PHONE? Where? He pointed to an alcove in the wall of the restaurant , and we ran to it. It was international, and I always had a bunch of change.

Lawrence talked with Federico and was told to call back in an hour. OK, Carlos was saying that he could find us a hotel in Aguas Calientes, not to worry, but it would cost us $100 US dollars for his services. His brother had a hotel there, "A very nice hotel," and he could make arrangements. He would give us the address and his brother's name.

It was around 1:00 p.m., and Carlos told us that he could call his brother, give us a tour of the ruins, we could take the bus down the mountain, check in at the hotel, and even visit the Aguas Calientes hot springs. This sounded good, and we told him we'd let him know after the call to Federico.

We did the tour and went back to the restaurant for a snack, a call to Federico, and to make our decision.

"I do not know what has happened with your plans. The hotel in Cusco, the train, and now the hotel at the top. There is nothing that I can do to change this very unfortunate situation," Federico said. "The plan that you have sounds OK, but call me when you are in the hotel in Aguas Calientes."

2:30 p.m.: Pay Carlos for helping us, go down the mountain on the bus. There's the boy on every downward grade, "Heeel-loooooooo!" Money out the windows, yaaaay!

We made it down and to the bus stop, out and walking to the town.

3:15 p.m.: I had the address of the hotel, but I didn't see any "nice hotel" anywhere and the town was small. I stopped a passerby and showed him the address. He smiled and said, "Dos cuadras, por alla," then points up the dirt pathway. We walked the two blocks and there was a single-story concrete building that said HOSTAL. I was feeling a bit HOSTILE by this time, especially when we walked in and it smelled like putrefied urine.

We walked up to the desk, the whole entourage of ten, and Carmen asked (in Spanish), "Disculpe, hay un hotel aqui?"

"No, senorita, no hay hoteles aqui. Solo esta hostal. Es siete Soles por persona."

I'm sure you probably got that conversation. No hotels in this town, just this, and it is seven soles per person.

I looked at Lawrence, he looked at me, we looked at the group, and I asked the receptionist if there was a pay phone here. Lawrence ran to it and called Federico, who said that he would make a call and to call back in an hour.

We paid, and the girls followed one arrow as we followed the other. *Mujeres, Varones,* Girls, Boys.

We had just enough time to walk to the hot springs. We threw our bags on the beds, ran out, and started up the path.

Uneventful. It was dirty, smelly, not maintained, but had a lot of backpacker traffic. Not a good combination.

5:30 p.m.: Darkness falling. We were almost to the hostal when two young men came running up to us, out of breath, yelling, "BISHOP! BISHOP!" Lord God, I thought, *Have we been delivered from HELL?* One of them spoke English and asked where our bags were. We all ran to the hostal, grabbed our gear, and hightailed it out of there.

We stumbled down the railroad tracks about a half of a mile, with the two boys helping with the heavier bags. They started up a cutoff, and I looked up to see an immaculate white stucco building with a terracotta tile roof.

We walked inside, sweating, out of breath, but relieved. The receptionist told us that the owner had called to have the staff "FIND THE BISHOP PARTY" in Aguas Calientes, and bring them back to the Pueblo Hotel. She asked what type of rooms we wanted. We booked four doubles, and two suites. Yes, we did have to pay, but at a discounted rate.

We found out later that Jose, owner of The Pueblo, was Federico's friend, and he pulled in a personal favor. And that is one of the reasons we love Federico Perez, this day and beyond.

All the rooms were beautiful, well maintained, but our suites were spectacular. King bed, fireplace, breakfast nook, and outside porch. It was very comfortable.

That night we went to have dinner in the hotel restaurant. The food, music, and service were all exquisite.

Lawrence, Norman, Federico at Yacumama Lodge, 1994

We spent the second day

at the ruins on our own, taking pictures and peeking a thousand feet down to the Urubamba River. Our kids seemed to really love it, and the mystic energy was captivating.

Machu Picchu ruins

On the way down the mountain, I think I figured it out. I wasn't sure, but I believe that the boy yelling, "Heeel-looooooooo!" grew three inches and looked a little older on some of the switchbacks. I guess it really doesn't matter, because it was still a grand feat for two boys to pull off, but with four boys...well, I don't know.

We were traveling back to Cusco in the morning, round-trip tickets, and we wanted to have a good time on our last night. Good music, good food, and good company.

Morning came too soon, and we stumbled back down the path to the train station. I mean, after all, it was 10:30 a.m., almost the crack of noon! You could sleep on the train if someone held you. We were climbing over 3,000 feet, back to Cusco.

They were saying that it would take longer since we were climbing the mountains, but what we were in for, no one could have guessed.

***

The view was incredible. A clear, sunny day where one could see the mountaintops, glaciers, rivers, and green valleys. On this trip we were able to sit close to one another and converse, so going up was much more enjoyable than going down.

About an hour and a half into the trip, it started feeling like we were going slower on the steep climbs, but I figured it was just my imagination. I kept telling myself that for about three climbs, then I had to face the fact that we were losing power or traction. By this time, 2:00 p.m., we were between Ollantaytambo and Urubamba, sort of in line with the salt mines, or the Moray Archaeological Site.

We were definitely slowing down, even on the flat planes, and I looked at the steward, showed my palms, and shrugged my shoulders. He looked at me, raised his eyebrows, and pursed his lips. I wasn't 100 percent sure, but I took it to mean that things were not right.

We limped into Urubamba at 4:00 p.m. We were supposed to be in Cusco by now. We sat in the train for another hour until they told us that the train had overheated and had problems with the engine. They had busses coming to transport us to Cusco. They should arrive shortly.

Shortly was almost 7:00 p.m. and darker than dark. Arriving in Cusco at almost 10:00 p.m. after a very rough mountain road trip, we were just glad that it had been dark and we couldn't see the road. Happy to be going to the hotel, we were whistling all the way.

With nothing to eat all day but snack crackers and sugar sodas, we searched out food, returned to the hotel, and slept in our single beds. Carmen and I only had one single bed in our room, and there was hot water for one hour in the morning. Machu Picchu felt like Florida compared to this 28-degree Cusco.

***

In the morning we did a bit of shopping—llama wool sweaters, antique woven goods, chullo hats, Peruvian mountain style. We ate at a cool restaurant, returned to the hotel, packed up, headed off to the airport, flew to Lima, checked in at the hotel, we ate, we slept, and the next day, everyone left us. Just like that. Carmen and I flew to Iquitos together to caaaaarry on, and we did!

To be continued...

Please watch for
CHASING THE DREAM
Ten Years in the Upper Amazon
Book Two

COMING SOON

Read about the trials and tribulations of fraud, theft, and bribery. The joy and jubilation of hosting large numbers of tourists (eco tourists, children's groups, medical, and scientific groups) at our Yacumama Lodge. Experience tussles with the Jungle Fishing Mafia, poachers, a Colombian cocaine cartel, the Iquitos justice system (an oxymoron), and much, much more…

Read a special sneak peek of
Chasing the Dream on page 266.

ACKNOWLEDGMENTS

A very special thank you to Emily Hitchcock and Steven Shephard, and to everyone who has touched my life through these honing years. You all are "Jewels, among the broken shells, in the Museum of My Life." The list is too long, and you know who you are. That is what is important, and I love you all.

P.S. Please forgive me if I have made mistakes and write like a novice, for I am only learning how to fly.

ABOUT THE AUTHOR

Norman Walters was born and grew up on Midwestern farmland soil in Mishawaka and Goshen, Indiana. He is a musician, songwriter, and artist, performing and exhibiting around the USA since his teenage years. Walters attended art school in Fort Wayne, Indiana, and has created many unusual careers and businesses. The last one, Yacumama Lodge in Peru, his inspiration to begin writing, is just another facet carved in this gem called LIFE.

If you'd like to know more about Norman Walters and his many adventures, visit him at www.normanwalters.com, or Google Norman Walters/Yacumama Lodge.

A host of information and articles about Yacumama Lodge can be found on the internet, and at www.yacumamalodge.net.

If you have specific research requests, the author welcomes and encourages inquiries and can be reached directly at newaltersdesigns@gmail.com.

CHASING THE DREAM: A SNEAK PEEK

It was the early days of 1993 on the Río Yarapa, where we were situated 110 miles by speedboat, or about seventy-one miles as the heron flies up the Río Amazonas, from the jungle metropolis of Iquitos, Peru—one of the largest Amazon Rainforest jungle cities in the world. Iquitos has no roads in, and is only accessible from the outside world by water or air. It was here that I was contemplating the construction progress of our new project, YACUMAMA LODGE.

The incredible beginning of the main building

The lodge was the brainchild of Lawrence Bishop. Lawrence and I had been partners in adventure for close to twenty-five years, and at that time, our newest venture was constructing an ecologically sustained tourist facility in the middle of the Amazon Jungle.

I'm talking, deep, dark, primeval forest, where most of the

Native South American *Ribereños* (people who live on the banks of rivers) live in *tambos* and travel in dugout canoes. Rustic, baby!

I had hired ninety-six of these men and women to work with me, building the structural design. What they didn't know, I taught them, and what I didn't know, they taught me. The design was sort of Thai, with peaked roofs and openings for light and air circulation. These men, for the most part, built only with their machetes. I supplied hammers, saws, post-hole diggers, shovels, rakes, and crowbars to augment their abilities and diminish the construction time. It worked well, and four young men, whom I deemed able to learn the electric tools, became my assistants. Some of the men had a little schooling, and a few had finished high school in a larger pueblo, or town.

Finished main buildings, much later. Design completed.

Like I was saying, I was contemplating the progress of construction, sitting in my makeshift office area, when I heard, "Señor Norman, Señor Norman, BONES!"

I felt and heard someone running toward me on the wooden *pasadizo* (walkway), and lo and behold, into my office bursts my trusty site supervisor/translator, Esteban. He was talking very fast and appeared to be excited or alarmed.

"They were digging the corner post holes for your house porch, and they uncovered BONES, HUMAN BONES," he exclaimed. "Come, come, you must see. They say this is the site of an ancient cemetery."

That definitely brought me out of my reverie. Human bones were not what you wanted to find under your house in the Amazon jungle. Isn't that something you'd see in a movie? Wait a minute... breathe.

I tried to calm him down, and said, "Show me!"

As we walked down the pasadizo, Esteban relayed what the men were saying:

Tunchis, the name the local people gave the ghosts of their ancestors, were all around the burial sites. Because this particular location was probably part of history that was not in memory range, it was hard to tell who these Tunchis were. Tunchis could be helpful or destructive, depending on what our intentions were. The people of Puerto Miguel (the village closest to us, where we procured all the workers), had many verbally documented sightings of Tunchis in their current cemetery, across the river from the village.

OK. Got it! Now I just had to figure out what to do with this new information.

When we walked up to the site, nine men were standing as still as statues around the freshly dug hole that was twelve inches in diameter. Lying on the ground, exposed to the late-twentieth century elements, was a broken piece of bone. I knelt down to get a better look, and sure enough, it was the knee joint end of a human femur. This was not the direction I had anticipated us heading, but we were here and the men were spooked.

I told Esteban, "Return the bone fragment to its rightful resting place (the hole), fill the hole, and I will change the location of the house porch. We will not dig here again."

That seemed to ease some of the fear I had seen in the eyes of the men. I smiled at them, steepled my hands in prayer, turned, walked away, and hoped that they would continue working.

They did, but when I saw Juan (my old go-to guy), I told him about the occurrence and he had a very strange warning for me.

Apparently, when he was younger, he'd had a bad experience with Tunchis in a jungle village. When he recounted his experience later, an old man advised him to always sleep with his machete under his pillow. Touching the machete is a show of force, and scares the Tunchis away.

From that day forward, I've slept with my machete and my .38-caliber revolver under my pillow while in the jungle.

I was interested in this aspect of the jungle because I was interested in the spirit world. I'd had a few unexplained occurrences in my life that could only be explained through spirit meddling. My mom, sister, and I were transfixed by the Ouija board in the mid-1960s. We were attempting contact with the spirit world and received a bunch of conflicting responses. That didn't stop us, though, and we proceeded until lack of interest set in.

***

I had been living in my house on the river for some time, concentrating on the construction, when Lawrence's brother John and his wife Yamuna came to Peru to lend a helping hand. John, having carpentry skills, and Yamuna, managerial/cooking skills, fit in perfectly with our plans.

I'll tell you, it was great having someone to converse with in English. I had been on my own for about eight months after the initial push with Lawrence in late 1992. My girlfriend, Carmen (who didn't speak English yet), and Yamuna got along really well. Carmen's three-year-old daughter, Naylita, was the ice breaker for all of us. So cute.

One night, while John, Yamuna and I were sitting around talking, the conversation turned to the digging up of bones. You know, a very common topic. They were also very interested.

Yamuna asked, "Have you had any strange feelings, like heard or seen anything?"

"Well, I have to say that it is pretty dead around here in the night, as you have found to be true, I'm sure," I responded.

"That a pun or what?" John asked.

"Just kidding, John. It is loud, but silent. If you know what I mean?"

"Yes, the cacophony, when you tune it out, is jungle silence, and it is almost deafening," added Yamuna, smiling.

We finished socializing and I strolled off down the pasadizo to my casa. I typed for a while on my old Royal portable typewriter, logging events in the hope of writing books about my experiences in the Amazon.

I did all the things a person does when getting ready to be unconscious for seven hours—changing into jammies, brushing teeth, shooing the mosquitos away from the bed, dropping and tucking the net in around the mattress, grabbing my book, and climbing into the sleep chamber. I read a chapter or two in the book *The Farm on the River of Emeralds*, turned the kerosene lamp down to a flicker, and surrendered to the inevitable.

Not long after, I heard noises in the silence, almost like ropes being dragged down the pasadizo and whispered phrases I couldn't make out. I just figured the night watchman was sweeping or something. The noises got louder, and I decided to raise myself up to see what the commotion was all about. I was going to push my body up with my right arm, but to my surprise, it felt like it was glued to the bed. I tried to move my body, and it was glued also.

Now, either some butt crazy witch doctor had blown curare powder up my nose, or I was dead or dreaming. My mind wasn't sending signals anymore, but my eyes were open and I was aware of my surroundings. It had to be the curare, and I was Wade Davis in *The Serpent and the Rainbow.*

I struggled, using all of my strength and might, but it was to no avail, for I felt paralyzed. I then noticed that the scraping and murmuring voices were at my door, and I could actually see shadows milling around through the screen. The door did not open, but the shadowy figures were appearing inside my room and moving toward the center of the floor.

All of a sudden, a thought entered my mind. *The machete!* Juan had told me to grab the machete. I forced, forced harder, and forced ever harder yet. My hand moved. I looked up, and saw the forms start to encircle my bed, swaying slightly, like they were floating. I continued forcing my will into my muscles, and I could feel the actual pressure that I was generating in my body. *Holy shit, could I have a coronary, or a stroke?* I looked up again, and dear Jesus, there were a lot of them starting to brush the mosquito net as they floated around the bed, coming closer and closer, and only one of me. But my hand kept moving, slowly, but centimetering along.

What really bothered me was the murmuring, whispered words, not discernible, in no real idiom, and the strange musty smell. It was just plain creepy. I felt the mosquito net begin to stretch inward, and looking out of the corner of my eye at my hand, saw that I was there.

I grabbed the handle, and everything that had been occurring, d i s a p p e a r e d ! Poof, just like that, gone. I looked around, machete in hand, parted the mosquito net, exited the sleep chamber, turned up the lamp, checked the bathroom, every corner, and then…walked out the door of my house.

I hurried down the pasadizo, found our security man, Frank, led him to Esteban's cabin, woke him up and asked, "Were there any people moving around tonight, on the walkway?"

"No, Señor, nadie. Todo estaba en silencio," responded Frank, looking at me. He added, "Por que?"

Supposedly everything was quiet. Frank was looking at me in a very queer way and had asked me why I was asking.

I asked Esteban to tell him there was no reason, that I thought that I had heard something, and that was all. "Buenas noches."

"Goodnight to all," I murmured to myself, walking back to my house. Boy oh boy. Either I was really out of it, dreaming, or Juan was right. In my gut, I knew the truth. Tunchis. I have never told anyone the whole story. I guess I was waiting for the books to begin.

Please watch for

CHASING THE DREAM

Ten Years in the Upper Amazon
Book Two

COMING SOON

www.ingramcontent.com/pod-product-compliance
Lightning Source LLC
LaVergne TN
LVHW041540070426
835507LV00011B/834